Praise for *Natural Meditation*

"If you thought you didn't have the time, focus, or discipline to meditate, this book is for you. The approach is both simple and fun, but don't be fooled. It's powerful because it's doable—and truly transformative."

—LISA OZ, host, *The Lisa Oz Show*

"Dean Sluyter is in the grand tradition of authors who interpret traditional enlightenment teachings and apply them to modern Western life. This book accomplishes that task with a rare combination of insight, clarity, wit, and pragmatic common sense."

—PHILIP GOLDBERG, author, *American Veda: From Emerson and the Beatles to Yoga and Meditation*

"If you were going to read one book on meditation, this would be the one."

—SHIVA REA

"I've attended Dean's sessions, and this book captures their spirit: relaxed and accessible, with a pop culture–tinged playfulness that pulls you in and puts you at ease."

—LISA LEEMAN, producer, *Crazy Wisdom*, and codirector, *Awake: The Life of Yogananda*

"With simplicity, wit, and clarity, Dean Sluyter debunks the misconceptions and offers a user-friendly practice that will put you in the 'Ahhhhhhh' space, regardless of circumstances. He is truly the Wizard of Ahhhhhhhs. This book will help you find the spacious grace in your life."

—STEVE BHAERMAN, aka Swami Beyondananda, author and cosmic comic

"Dean Sluyter dispels many myths about meditation with clarity, eloquence, and insight. Without recourse to spiritual cliche or jargon, he shows that meditation is natural and effortless, and can be practiced by anyone who simply wishes to avail themselves of the peace that lies in the depths of their being at all times and under all circumstances."

—RUPERT SPIRA, author, *Presence* and *The Ashes of Love*

Also by Dean Sluyter

Why the Chicken Crossed the Road
and Other Hidden Enlightenment Teachings

The Zen Commandments:
Ten Suggestions for a Life of Inner Freedom

Cinema Nirvana:
Enlightenment Lessons from the Movies

JEREMY P. TARCHER/PENGUIN
a member of Penguin Group (USA)
New York

Natural
Meditation

A Guide to Effortless
Meditative Practice

Dean Sluyter

JEREMY P. TARCHER/PENGUIN
Published by the Penguin Group
Penguin Group (USA) LLC
375 Hudson Street
New York, New York 10014

USA · Canada · UK · Ireland · Australia
New Zealand · India · South Africa · China

penguin.com
A Penguin Random House Company

Most Tarcher/Penguin books are available at special quantity discounts for bulk
purchase for sales promotions, premiums, fund-raising, and educational needs.
Special books or book excerpts also can be created to fit specific needs.
For details, write: Special.Markets@us.penguingroup.com.

Library of Congress Cataloging-in-Publication Data

Sluyter, Dean.
Natural meditation : a guide to effortless meditative practice / Dean Sluyter.
p.   cm.
Includes index.
ISBN 978-0-399-17141-3
1. Meditation.   1. Title.
BL627.S59   2015   2014039692
158.1'2—dc23

Printed in the United States of America
1   3   5   7   9   10   8   6   4   2

Book design by Lauren Kolm

For Yaffa

. . . i and i . . . sky into sky . . .

Contents

Where there is effortlessness, there is peace.

—*Sri Mooji*

1. Meditation for the Rest of Us

Please try this:

Turn your head to the left. See whatever you see.

Now turn your head to the right. See whatever you see.

OK. You saw two different views, but what remained the same?

Now scrunch up your shoulders into an awkward position. Feel whatever you feel.

Then drop them back into a comfortable position, and feel whatever you feel.

Two different feelings, but what remained the same?

What *always* remains the same?

Please recall leaning forward to blow out the candles on (let's say) your seventh birthday cake. There were the glowing flames filling your visual field . . . their warmth against your face . . . the sound of your family shouting, "Make a wish!" . . . the smell of sugary icing and melting wax . . . the feeling of being inside a highly excited seven-year-old body.

Now recall hanging out with friends at seventeen. All the sights and smells and sounds were different: maybe cigarettes . . . beer . . . pizza . . . wisecracks . . . loud music. You had a different voice, and you were in a different body, one with hair in new places and prone to recurring storms of sexual arousal. Your range of emotions was very different, with levels of sarcasm and romantic desperation unknown at age seven. But what remained the same?

And now please recall the last argument you were in. Recall eating dinner yesterday. Falling asleep last night. Opening this book a few moments ago. Different, different, different. But what remains the same?

Here's a hypothesis:

No matter how much our experiences change, one thing always remains the same: the presence of an experiencing awareness, which we call "I."

Running through every moment of your life, whether you're perceiving your senior prom or your retirement party, is that one thread—the conscious presence that's there to perceive it all, the sense of an awareness or "I," the simple knowingness by which all these impressions are known, right now and always. It's just yourself, and it's self-evident.

Now, do you have one special I-awareness to experience the view to your left and a different one for the right? Is there one for the awkward feeling when you scrunch your shoulders and one that takes over when you relax them? Clearly not. (To confirm that, scrunch up one shoulder while you leave the other one down.) So it's also self-evident that it's the *same* awareness, the same I that experiences everything, at every moment and at every age, even as the body, thoughts, and feelings incessantly change. Awareness is the constant; everything else is variable.

No one had to teach you this I-sense. It was there before you knew your name or knew you were a boy or a girl. It's there as the silent witness of your dream adventures and your waking adventures, and it's there whether you're depressed or happy, agitated or tranquil, so sick you can't remember how it felt to be healthy or so healthy you can't remember how it felt to be sick. You don't have to do anything to create or maintain it. In fact, see if you can get rid of it.

No?

So here's the method . . . the meditation:

Rest in the I-sense.

That's it.

Just bring your attention to this always-present experience of being aware. Don't worry about the things you're aware *of*, which come and go. Since you don't need to hang on to this I-sense—since you can't get rid of it—there's little or nothing to do. You can sit or stand, walk or lie down, with eyes open or closed. You don't have to push away thoughts; they come and go, and the I is there to perceive them. You don't have to relax; relaxation and tension come and go, but *you* remain as their silent witness, unchanged by either.

Please do this for a few moments right now, just resting in the already-present I-sense. After a while you'll "stop." That is, you'll start reading again or go on to do something else . . . but of course the I-awareness will be perceiving that as well.

~

Why is this important?

Please imagine a perfect moment—whatever that would be for you. You've just surfed a thirty-footer off the north coast of Maui . . . or crushed the LSAT . . . or hit the jackpot in Atlantic City . . . or enjoyed a delicious dinner at an excellent restaurant with a lovely new romantic prospect. You've got money in the bank, none of your body parts hurt, and you're having a great hair day. There's a feeling that we can only describe as . . . *Ahhhhhhh!*

But then the next wave knocks the wind out of you, you swallow water, and you scratch your face all over the bottom . . . or you're not sure you want to go to law school after all . . . or you lose all your winnings at the craps table . . . or you get a weird call from your date the next morning . . . or that itchy patch of skin is flaring up again, or you're depressed again, or you've got that annoying insurance commercial stuck in your head.

How long does ahhhhhhh ever last? The problem is that it's always dependent on so many shifting, changing circumstances, from your date's mood to the surf report. It's all (as Paul Simon sang) slip slidin' away.

What has probably brought you to this book is the suspicion that somehow there's an *inner* ahhhhhhh that doesn't depend on your luck, your accomplishments, your health, or anything else, and that it can be found through meditation. Your suspicion is correct. I've seen people find that ahhhhhhh after losing everything in an earthquake, or while they're serving a thirty-year sentence in a prison where they don't even have the luxury of a private toilet stall. And I've seen people find it in the comfort of the suburbs. Anyone can find it, because it's the overlooked nature of our own basic awareness, the I-sense that everyone has and no one can get rid of.

There's just one hitch: it's hard to believe it can be that easy.

It's like computers. Before 1984, most people thought of them as powerful in some vague, mysterious way, but forbidding, weird, a little scary. Computers were something for a different kind of person to operate, an alien breed of supergenius science geeks. And, in fact, most computers back then did run on arcane "line commands" or "dot commands": to indent a paragraph, you might have to type something like ".x703." The screen displays were blocky, squint-inducing green characters on a black background, always in that same clumsy typewriter font.

Then Apple introduced Macintosh, the easy-to-use "computer for the rest of us." In the ads, its squat, upright shape and its gently rounded edges made it look like R2-D2, the cutest little robot in the galaxy. Off to the right was the newfangled point-and-click mouse thingy, with its tail in a gentle curve. In black letters on a soft-white screen was a sentence of just one word, ending with a period but starting with a grammar-defying lowercase letter. And, impossibly, it was written in a cursive font, like the handwriting of a warm, chummy, understandable human:

hello.

Oh! Computers could be friendly. They could be like humans. They could be *for* humans, regular humans, the rest of us, the ungeeks, the non–rocket scientists. We could do this.

The aim of this book is to welcome you, with the same kind of hello, to user-friendly meditation: meditation for the rest of us. Despite its growing popularity, many people still think of meditation as powerful in some vague, mysterious way, but forbidding, weird, a little scary. It's for a different kind of person, an alien breed of—hmmm, let's see—maybe monks who live austere lives of grueling concentration, or maybe touchy-feely Californians who listen to tinkling chimes while they eat granola and massage one another with crystals, or maybe just people with some kind of extraordinary commitment that the rest of us lack.

Actually, those stereotypes contain a grain of truth. Most approaches to meditation are, we could say, either "hard" or "soft." The hard methods do require a lot of concentration, a struggle to control thoughts and "tame the mind." They're like bitter medicine; you hold your nose, gulp it down, and hope you'll eventually feel better. The soft methods might involve some feel-good visualization or trippy New Age music or efforts to cultivate only happy-face, positive emotions . . . even if it kills you. This approach is like sweet, syrupy medicine that may be popular ("Kids love it!") but doesn't do much for you.

But these two seemingly opposite approaches have something fundamental in common. They're both unnatural. Something inside us understands that, and rebels against their artificiality, which is precisely why sticking to them *does* require extraordinary commitment. As a result, I meet a lot of people who tell me that they've tried meditation, but (guilty eye-roll here) "I had trouble sticking to it" or "I guess I just don't have the discipline."

Good news: you're not the problem.

If we eliminate both the hard and the soft, the two unnatural approaches, what's left? *Natural* meditation—as natural as breathing, walking, laughing, or being the I that you already are. This is meditation for the rest of us. As you've seen, it's straightforward. There's no straining to concentrate, or cop a "spiritual" attitude, or imitate someone else's lifestyle. Because it's natural, it's easy to learn and do. Meditation is supposed to make life smoother, less stressed, more friction-free, more like open sky, less like sand in your bathing suit. If the process of meditation itself makes you *more* stressed, then (as De Niro says in *Raging Bull*) it defeats its own purpose.

"But I've tried to meditate, and it was difficult."

The key word here is *tried*. What, exactly, were you trying to do? Please spell that out; put it into a sentence. If you try to lift your chair with one finger or try to fly around the room, it's very clear what you're trying to do, and that it's something difficult. *Whatever it was you were trying to do in the name of meditation, you don't have to do.* It was just some misunderstanding, or some *un*natural meditation instruction, that led you to believe you had to do it. As you'll see, meditation is not doing, but being. And being is effortless—it's unavoidable.

Effortless doesn't mean watered down. I didn't make up this stuff; its pedigree is long and distinguished. I've had the privilege of training directly with some of the pre-eminent teachers on the planet, and I've applied what I've learned from them seriously (though not solemnly), sometimes on retreats for months at a stretch. I've observed its effects in my own life and in other people's lives since the Johnson administration. I know it works.

We'll take it step by step, and we'll go at a relaxed pace. I'll introduce a number of specific natural meditative techniques, and you'll develop a sense of which ones you most strongly gravitate toward. We'll discuss the points of practice as well as the *results* of practice as they begin to surface in daily life. Your questions—that is, the questions that people have asked repeatedly over the last umpty-ump years—will be answered.

As with learning to tie your shoes, it might seem a bit puzzling at first, but with a little practice and encouragement, pretty soon it's a matter of "Oh yeah . . . this!" and then you do it almost without thinking about it. I suggest that you try the methods in the sequence presented, as the earlier experiences prepare the ground for the later ones. But ultimately feel free to use whatever resonates for you, whatever you find helpful, and don't worry about the rest. Take your time. When you feel you've really connected with one of the methods, there's no need to rush on to the next. Any one of them can provide rich growth for days or years.

We'll draw on several wisdom traditions without being locked into any one of them. One of my first teachers was fond of saying, "The knowledge that is in the book remains in the book"; it's in the *living* that these teachings prove out. So I'll illustrate many of the points with stories of my own thrills and spills and those of others. Stories are fun, but they also help keep things grounded in actuality rather than drifting off into academic theory or spiritual fantasyland. There's no need to go woo-woo. The actuality of this stuff as it unfolds in your life is deeper than any woo. It's *Whoa!* It's *Ahhhhhhh!*

~

I'm writing this on the little deck in my garden, occasionally serenaded by a mockingbird or buzzed by a hummingbird. Feel free to imagine that you're sitting here with me on a lazy afternoon, that this is where our sharing takes place.

I think there are many people who feel pulled toward meditation but are held back by the notion that it lies on the other side of some narrow door, and that passing through the door requires a lot of work, or study, or discipline, or belief, or ceremony, or money, or finding the one "right" teacher or technique out of a bewildering array of choices. But I can promise you that the door is wide open and easy to pass through. By the time you finish this book, in fact, you'll see that the door is everywhere. You'll feel thoroughly at home doing one simple, crucial thing: relaxing into the rich silence at the center of your being. And you'll discover that it heals and nurtures every area of your life.

2. Unexpect the Expected

Here's a conversation I've had about a hundred times, in various forms, when meeting a new acquaintance at a social gathering:

NEW ACQUAINTANCE: "So . . . what do you do?"

ME: "Oh, I write and I teach meditation."

NEW ACQUAINTANCE: "Meditation? Jeez, I could never do that. I can't concentrate to save my life."

ME: "Me neither."

Pause.

NEW ACQUAINTANCE: "Have you tried the shrimp?"

Or:

"So . . . what do you do?"

"I write and I teach meditation."

"Meditation? Boy, that must take a lot of discipline."

"No, not really."

Pause.

"Have you tried the shrimp?"

Or:

"Meditation? I'm not the type—too fidgety."
"Actually, I've taught a lot of fidgety adolescents and convicts. They do fine with it."
Pause.
"Have you tried the shrimp?"

I don't try to push these conversations any further, not being a pushy guy. (And besides, I want to get to the shrimp before it's gone.) But the fact is that many people have preconceptions about meditation that have little to do with the reality of the thing. And when new evidence doesn't square with our old opinions, we're often more comfortable sticking with our old opinions. (That's certainly true, for instance, in politics.)

So, when you're trying to communicate what something is, it's often easier if you first eliminate what it isn't. Imagine trying to teach someone to ride a bike, someone who's convinced it requires them to wave their arms around wildly. Or imagine going to a play and bringing your own program, one you've made yourself, based on what, for some reason, you *think* you're going to see. Onstage, the action may be unfolding beautifully, but if you keep looking down from the play to your program and trying to reconcile the two, you're going to get confused. "Wait a minute . . . where's the part where Hamlet meets Juliet?"

I invite you, then, to burn your program—to unexpect the expected.

If you never meditated before opening this book, your program is based on what you've heard or read or speculated. Burn it, please. If you've done other forms of meditation, your program is also based on whatever you were taught (or *thought* you were taught), and whatever you ran into while practicing it. In that case . . . burn, baby, burn. What we do here will be simpler and easier than what you did before; if you try to filter the new stuff through your memories of the old stuff, it's going to introduce needless complications.

In either case, to help you burn your program thoroughly, let me point out some of the most common expectations. All of them, as you'll see, turn out not to be true of natural meditation.

SOME EXPECTATIONS:

Meditation is hard.

It requires you to concentrate and make your mind a blank.

It requires a spiritual attitude. (Whatever that is.)

It makes people passive and apathetic.

Meditation can be done only by mellow, relaxed people. (Can you see
    the backward logic of this one? It's like saying only people with a full
    tank can stop for gas.)

There's only one right meditation technique.

You'll have to master *lots* of meditation techniques.

It takes a long time to get results.

It's not for you because you _____. (Fill in the
    blank: have kids, work nights, play football, play the stock market,
    whatever.)

It conflicts with your religion.

It's only a form of relaxation, like getting a massage.

It won't help *your* problems.

It will magically and immediately solve *all* your problems.

To meditate, you need silence.

To meditate, you need a mantra.

To meditate, you need to be a vegetarian.

You need to believe in karma, or dharma, or some version of Eastern philosophy.

You need a guru.

You need a cushion.

You need solitude. (As you'll see, meditation can be a great workplace skill.)

You need to sit in a difficult position.

You need to sit with your eyes closed. (Even that's not necessarily true.)

We could go on. So whatever concepts you may have picked up along the way, please just drop them for now. Don't take my word that they're mistaken. Just burn your program and *see* what actually happens on the stage.

That's called the scientific method, and it's what great sages, both Eastern and Western, have advised for centuries. Socrates roamed the streets of Athens, engaging people in probing dialogues that systematically deconstructed their stale concepts till they fell apart; then they could look with fresh eyes. Seng-ts'an, the third Zen patriarch, said, "Do not seek truth; merely cease to cherish opinions." Both the Old and New Testaments are filled with prophets saying, "Lo and behold!"—that is, "Look and see!" And the Buddha said:

> Do not believe a thing because many repeat it. Do not accept a thing on the authority of one or another of the sages of old, nor on the ground that a statement is found in the books. . . . After examination, believe that which you have tested for yourselves.

Part of the problem is the word *meditation*. That's a big word—four syllables. It sounds as if the thing it describes must be a big, arduous task. And everyone has their own associations with the word, whether it's bells and incense or stained glass and organ music. When you drop all those associations, what's left? If it were up to me, I'd do away with that word entirely, but then what would go on the cover of this book? The Tibetans have a much smoother, mellower word for it: *gompa*. And they're so clear that it's not about gritting your teeth and banging your head against the wall of your cave that they have a saying: *Gompa ma yin, kompa yin.* "Meditation isn't, acclimation is." It's so simple and natural that there's ultimately nothing to do; it's just a matter of acclimating to doing nothing. I know, that's hard to believe . . . till you get a little taste and you lo and behold it for yourself.

It may also be a bit less unbelievable if you have a sense that the person saying it has some kind of qualifying background, so I suppose I should mention that I've been at this for most of my life. When I was five or six I started asking the deep life questions that most kids ask—but I never stopped. By the time I was seventeen, I was in full exploration mode: hanging out in San Francisco with the local Zen masters, dancing with the Sufi masters, chanting with Swami Bhaktivedanta at the Hare Krishna temple, and singing and dancing through the Sabbath with Rabbi Shlomo Carlebach and his joyous band of hippie Hasidim. Hey, it was 1967, and San Francisco was a seeker's feast.

My early, brief forays into Zen turned out to be instructive in a backhanded way. I'd always been a fidgety type (like those adolescents and convicts), and the Zen teachers expected me to sit motionless, like a Buddha statue, for long periods. If my nose itched or my knee ached, I had to tough it out. I was also supposed to be doing some very intense concentration, which, again, is not in my bag of tricks. To this day, I have great respect for the sit-like-a-rock stillness of Zen practitioners, but I could see I wasn't going to be one of them.

So I moved on, and I found teachers who showed me that there are ways to meditate that are more suited to the rest of us—natural, relaxed, human ways. They showed me that we don't have to impose stillness on the body and mind. We *are* the stillness that *underlies* body and mind, the innate I-sense that just needs to be noticed. For some years I practiced Transcendental Meditation with Maharishi Mahesh Yogi, then moved on to explore Vajrayana Buddhist methods with a number of lamas, the devotional approach of Bhakti Yoga, and the penetrating self-inquiry of Advaita Vedanta. I went on pilgrimages and long retreats in the United States, Europe, India, Nepal, and Tibet.

Several of my teachers encouraged me to teach, which I did, from Los Angeles to Philadelphia to New Orleans (where one of my talks was drowned out by an early Mardi Gras parade) to Iowa to Las Vegas. I landed in New Jersey for a few decades, where I raised a family, taught English and meditation at a top-drawer prep school, and volunteered as a chaplain (aka meditation teacher) at a maximum-security prison. On and off I've led courses and workshops at conferences, universities, yoga studios, and retreat centers throughout the U.S.

My life has been very, very lucky. I've had a chance to learn from sages in a variety of traditions and to identify the distilled essence of their teaching: simple, natural nondoing, the delicious ease of just being. I've practiced it through easy times and hard times, including serious illness, romantic crises, and the deaths of people closest to me. And through my teaching, I've had a chance to see that it works just as well for teenagers and grandparents, valedictorians and grade-school drop-outs, indie filmmakers and corporate samurai.

Now, when we say "It works," what do we mean? What does it do? Certainly relaxation, energy, mental clarity, patience, centeredness, freedom from stress and various dependencies . . . all those benefits do tend to accrue. But they're really symptoms of something bigger:

The way you experience your life in each moment is transformed.

What exactly is that like? Well, rather than create a whole new set of expectations, we'll explore that in detail as you start to practice and your own experiences naturally unfold. I want you to test it, to lo and behold it yourself.

For now, though, we can say this:

Remember, when you were a kid, the feeling of being "in trouble"? *Dum-da-dum-dum!* That sinking, overwhelming, all-is-lost feeling of hopeless, inescapable, irredeemable doom? This is the opposite . . . permanently.

Or we can say this:

Perhaps you've had the frustrating experience of trying to get some gadget or appliance to work. You keep punching different buttons in different combinations till suddenly, "D'oh!"—you realize you skipped Step 1: "Be sure power cord is connected to wall socket." We've been trying to get our *lives* to work, but we've skipped Step 1. We need to connect to the power source: our basic beingness, our unmoved aware-ness, our real self. Then a whole lot of frustrated punching of a whole lot of buttons drops away.

And we can say this:

Gradually—and sometimes not so gradually—that inner ahhhhhhh we spoke of grows clearer and clearer, and abides longer and longer. One day it becomes like a light that's so steady it can never go out, so brilliant it pervades and illuminates every bit of your life. Then people give it names like awakening, transcendence, enlightenment, self-realization, *moksha*, nirvana, *hashra'ah*, *fanaa*, the kingdom of heaven within.

But don't let the exotic names throw you. What they point to is the core of your own being, more intimate than your own breath, more natural than the flow of these words through your consciousness right now. It's just been temporarily overlooked. Our project together is to stop overlooking it.

3. Meditating on a Single Breath

In Chapter 1, we learned to rest in the I-sense. Now let's explore another very simple yet potent technique. As with all the methods we'll be learning, I suggest that you first read the instructions in a leisurely, unhurried way, lightly imagining yourself doing what's being described. Then put the book aside and do it. Afterward, you can look over the instructions again. Don't worry about whether you're remembering everything you read, or doing it "right." When little kids play their made-up games, or great jazz musicians play their improvised flights, they don't worry about doing it right, and that's what *makes* it right. In any case, after one or two cycles of read/do/read/do, you'll have it down.

~

Sit comfortably. For now, don't worry about your exact position, or whether you're on a chair, couch, or cushion (or on a park bench, or a beach, or . . .). It's best not to sit in a rigidly erect posture and not to slouch; be somewhere comfortably between the two.

Close your eyes.

Lightly scan your body from the inside, and notice whether there are any parts that want to be loosened up somehow. You might want to do a few neck rolls in each direction, shrug your shoulders up toward your ears and then drop them, maybe twist your trunk to the left and to the right.

Then, just sit for a little while, letting everything be however it is. There's nothing for you to do about anything.

Now, take a single breath, in and then out.

(Of course, you've been breathing all along without necessarily noticing it. But now consciously take a single breath.)

Don't worry about whether it's deep or shallow, long or short—just a regular, natural breath.

Easily pay attention to what it's like—what you experience—as you breathe in.

Now pay attention to what you experience as you pause at the end of the in-breath. . . .

Now pay attention to what you experience as you breathe out. . . .

Now pay attention to what you experience as you pause at the end of the out-breath.

That's it. You're done.

Seriously, you're done. Just by leaving off focusing on outer matters for these few brief moments, by using just a single breath to lead your attention into this more inward space, you've done something quite significant. Out of the millions of breaths you'll take in this life, you've taken one consciously. You've thoroughly *inhabited* one. Most people go through the day without doing that, and many may go through a lifetime without doing that.

You're done.

Take your time opening your eyes.

Or...

Or you may not feel like opening your eyes just yet. You may notice that there's something that makes you feel like staying here, something naturally *attractive* about this inward direction.

If so, fine. *Now* take a single breath, again inhabiting it fully: paying easy attention to the in-breath, the pause at the end of the in-breath, the out-breath, and the pause at the end of the out-breath. *Now* you're done.

Or...

Or in case you *still* feel like staying put, *now* take a single breath . . .

And *now* . . .

And *now* . . .

Just taking a single breath.

Please note what you're *not* doing. You're not "practicing deep breathing." You're not "concentrating on the breath." You're certainly not "counting breaths." How can you count when you never go past one? It's always right now—never yesterday or tomorrow, never one second ago or one second from now—so you can never take more than a single breath. Anything before this breath is just a memory: that is, a thought. Anything after this breath is just anticipation: that is, a thought. We don't have to make a big deal about "nowness." There's nothing mysterious about it. It's the most ordinary thing in the world; in fact, it's all we have. We're *always* just taking a single breath, but now, for a change, we're paying attention to it.

As you take this single, present breath, notice where you feel it. Do you feel it only in the lungs? Do you feel it in your diaphragm? Do you feel it in your nostrils? In your throat? Your ribs? Your toes, somehow? The top of your skull, somehow? Not that you "should" necessarily feel it here or there. But notice what's actually felt, not just your offhand idea of it. Breathing is not just an idea. It's your experience. It's your life.

As we take the single breath, we're not trying to concentrate . . .

Not trying to clear the mind . . .

Not trying to block anything out . . .

Not trying to feel anything special . . .

Not trying to manipulate our experience in any way. We're just experiencing the breath, and whatever else happens or doesn't happen is fine.

Sometimes the breath may naturally become very deep and full, sometimes so light and subtle that it's barely perceptible. Sometimes the pauses at the end of the in-breath and out-breath may become quite long. Perfect. Just be with it, aware of it, however it is. You're the observer, the passenger, not driving, just along for the ride in the vehicle of breath.

Don't worry about the body getting enough oxygen. Because any settling down is spontaneous and not manipulated, even if you feel you're barely breathing it's fine. Thousands of people over thousands of years have safely logged millions of hours in this barely-breathing state.

As you breathe, awareness of sounds and other sensations will naturally be there. Thoughts and feelings will come and go. That's all fine— let them come and go. If at any point you realize that you've been off on some long train of thought, it doesn't matter. The moment you realize it, you're already off the train. That trip is already a memory, and your only concern is the single breath *now*.

Whatever feelings may come, of happiness or sadness, tranquillity or agitation, interest or boredom, or anything else, it's all fine. It doesn't matter what you think or feel. Just inhabit the single breath and don't much bother with whatever else is there. Consider it all background sounds. As when you're riding in a car or bus and talking with a friend, the background sounds are not a problem as long as you don't *make* them a problem.

It's all completely natural and straightforward—nothing forced, nothing strained. You're just breathing and experiencing; experiencing breathing. That simple.

When you decide you're really stopping for now, take a few minutes. Don't just jump up. Maybe slouch in your seat, change your position a little, then start to stretch and move your limbs a bit. You may feel like gently rubbing your hands, face, or scalp to get the circulation going again. After a while, start to crack the eyelids open a little, then take your time as you slowly open them all the way. Even if you feel you can come right out, always take at least a minute or two to ease out of meditation. You might even feel like lying down for a few minutes.

Then . . . dive back into your life and enjoy.

And note that at any time throughout the day—while sitting at a red light, at the beginning (or in the middle) of an important business meeting, when you're feeling stressed at the office, when you're feeling mellow in the park—you can use this method to access that meditative space, where you're naturally centered in nowness and in the simplicity of a single breath. In the middle of all the doing, you can always get back in touch with the core of just being. It's never more than a breath away—at most.

~

There's a saying that, just as scaling a mountain requires strong hands and feet to do the climbing as well as clear eyes to see the way ahead, so reaching the peak of enlightenment requires effective meditative practice as well as clear insight into where it's taking you. In that spirit, throughout this book we'll continue to alternate how-to chapters (like this one) with insight chapters (like the next one). As The Cat in the Hat says,

> It is fun to have fun
> But you have to know how.

4. Naturally

Congratulations—you're meditating! As much as anyone else, you've embarked on the meditative journey of fully opening your life. The important thing now is to maintain the momentum of that journey by continuing to practice, ideally every day, and to remember that the essence of the method is naturalness. This is a good time, then, to reflect a little more deeply on just what *natural* means—that is, what's in tune with nature.

Nature itself means a few things. One of them is the unspoiled outdoors. Not long ago, my wife and I took a trip to Mammoth Lakes, near Yosemite, and hiked up through the woods to McLeod Lake, which nestles at the foot of spectacular, craggy volcanic mountains. It was a sparkling, windless October day, and we were the only ones there. Silence. No cars, no airplanes, and at nine thousand feet not even a bird. Neither of us felt like speaking. But when we compared notes later, we both said how struck we were by the depth, the vibrancy of the silence.

In the world of radio and TV production, if two seconds go by without someone talking, it's called "dead air" and is to be avoided at all costs, no matter how frantically the hosts must jabber. But what we

experienced at McLeod Lake was what we might call *live* air: a reminder that silence is not flat and dry but juicy and alive. It's not just a
vacuum, not just the absence of motion and sound, but a fullness, a
fertile presence that is somehow the necessary background of motion
and sound . . . and perhaps, somehow, even its source.

Such experiences in the outdoors, in nature, are an echo of the
equally deep silence that's inside of us. If it weren't there, we couldn't
appreciate or even hear the outer silence. Whether you've encountered
it while hiking in the woods, or swimming in the ocean, or sinking your
hands into the soil in your own backyard—or, for that matter, while
strolling down the boulevard smoking a cigar—you know that this
inner silence, this live air, is not boring. It's not (as a lot of French phi-
losophers imagined) terrifying. And the great, amazing discovery is
that, because it's natural, it's always already there; it usually just goes
unnoticed. So when we meditate, we don't have to struggle to create it.
We just have to *recognize* it—tune in to it.

Usually, we act like radio hosts who are afraid they'll be fired if they
don't hold the dead air at bay in every moment. We fill our lives with
noise of all kinds, outer and inner. As soon as we start our cars, we turn
on the music. The moment there's a lull in the conversation, we whip
out our phones and check our messages. I like to walk at night. Most of
the people I see are walking their dogs, and these days most of them
have their heads down at that telltale forty-five-degree angle, their
faces bathed in the blue-gray glow of the cell phone, oblivious to the
quiet evening world that their dogs lead them through. (The dogs still
seem to enjoy it.)

Yet people travel hundreds of miles to places like Mammoth Lakes,
instinctively recognizing that the live-air silence has a healing, restor-

ative quality that our noisy lives require. And as we start to meditate and tune in more clearly to the natural silence that's always within us, we find that we're healed and restored on the fly, even as we engage in the noise and busyness of our everyday lives and responsibilities. You don't have to throw away your iPhone (although, in your own time, you may find yourself less compulsively addicted to it). But on the phone or off it, in the city or the mountains, you'll start to find that the mammoth silence is always with you.

Another aspect of nature is one that you can see—or, rather, hear—if you have, say, mockingbirds in your neighborhood. If you do, stop for a few minutes and listen to one sing. When it really gets cooking, you'll hear an amazing outpouring of song: an ever-changing stream of creative innovation to rival Jimi Hendrix, Keith Jarrett, John Coltrane, or any other great improvisational musician. Mockingbirds can't read music, don't attend music school, and never learn scales, but somehow they know how to just let the music happen. The flow of their music is not strained or contrived, because it's natural to them.

You can see a similar kind of flow if you walk beside a river or stream. Notice how it makes its course through the different elements it encounters. If you were to follow it closely as it goes through the rocks and marshes, the hard soil and the soft soil, till it arrives at the lake or ocean, you'd see that it flows in the most efficient way possible. The word *efficient*, especially the way it's used in the workaday world, might make us expect the stream to flow in a straight line—that's the shortest distance between two points, isn't it? If *we* were put in charge of directing streams, that might be how we'd do it. But then we would wind up dashing against the rocks and mountains in our path when we could more easily flow around them. Fortunately, Mother Nature is in charge, and Mother knows best. By not insistin

plan of a straight line, by adapting itself to w

point of its journey, the stream winds up mov

cient way possible—that is, it reaches its dest

least possible energy.

The behavior of the stream, in fact, reveals one of the most funda-mental laws of nature, one that shapes our entire universe. Called the *principle of least action,* it states that all the diverse phenomena we can observe, from galaxies to subatomic particles, are always doing as little as possible—always following the path of least resistance.

You see this law at work when you put a straw in a glass of water. It appears bent because water is denser than air; as the image of the submerged part travels to your eye, it lags behind that of the unsub-merged part because it refuses to do the extra work of moving through a denser medium at the same speed. It just says no. Pierre-Louis Mau-pertuis, the eighteenth-century mathematician who first described this law, summarized it by saying, "Nature is thrifty in all its actions." Or, be-cause nature always gets the most done with the least work, we could also say that it is *efficient* in all its actions—or lazy.

The consistency with which this principle works, at all places and times, is really quite amazing. When a drop of water falls, it spreads out as little as possible so that it doesn't have to tolerate any more surface tension than necessary. That's why, in a vacuum, it takes the shape of a perfect sphere. But when it falls through air, it adapts to the air's density, taking on a teardrop shape that's perfectly aerodynamic. And again, it does all this spontaneously, in real time, with no planning and no PhD in physics. The precise shape of every cloud you'll ever see, the size and speed of every planet's orbit around its star, the way the rios you ate for breakfast break down in your digestive tract, even chaotic, violent-looking phenomena like the eruption of a smoke-belching, lava-spewing volcano—it's all the workings (or shirkings) of the principle of least action, shaping the universe by moseying along in its own sweet time.

So let's take Mother Nature as our role model. If we're going to meditate (or do anything else) with all the power and ease of the universe behind us, we need to do it easily, naturally. The easy way is all around us, governing ants and earthquakes alike through the principle of least action. It's inside us, governing how our neurons fire and the blood moves through our veins. But we humans have a certain amount of free will—enough to choose the hard way, and we usually do. Perhaps that's what the story of the fall from the Garden of Eden is about: We start off in tune with nature, living a life of ease, but after a while, like an ornery two-year-old, we perversely shout "No!" Then (as John Goodman says in *The Big Lebowski*) we're entering a world of pain. And we've got to get ourselves back to the Garden.

There used to be a commercial with the punch line "It's not nice to fool Mother Nature!" It showed her in a cheesy white goddess costume, comically zapping some of her forest critters with a lightning bolt to punish them for passing off margarine as real butter. Every time we fool with Mother Nature by doing things the complicated, artificial way—the margarine way—we get burned. We stubbornly stick to our convoluted business plan for selling widgets in Madagascar, missing the easy market for wodgets in New Jersey; or we try to impose success on our kids with some trumped-up agenda that has nothing to do with their actual talents; or we try to squeeze our meditation experiences into the shape of some prefab concept. Sooner or later we'll see the light and let things be simple and easy again. Why not sooner? Whatever we're doing, we can make it hard or we can take it easy. Don't let the sound of your own wheels make you crazy.

But meditation is a big undertaking, isn't it? Isn't it going into a whole other state of consciousness or some such? Well, we go into another state of consciousness every night. It's called falling asleep, and nothing could be more natural. Even for insomniacs, sleep is eventually inevitable. Note the word *falling*. For everyone, falling is eventually inevitable; gravity is irresistible; the principle of least action makes falling easier than standing. Perhaps meditation could be called "falling awake."

But what's the gravity of meditation? To answer that question, please find something attractive—that is, something that attracts *you*. Go for a walk outside and find a flower, or a sunset, or a graceful building, or a good-looking babe or hunk walking by. Or just stay right where you are, look around the room you're in, and notice, perhaps, the rich, previously overlooked texture of the couch you're sitting on. Or put on your headphones and play some of your favorite music, or turn on the TV and watch your favorite show. Because the object is attractive, we enjoy it, and our attention naturally becomes absorbed in it. That's *our* nature. The principle of least action makes it easier to be absorbed in whatever we enjoy. *Joy is our gravity.* No one has to tell us to concentrate on something we like. We don't worry about whether our mind wanders. Sure, it does occasionally, but it keeps coming back, pulled by the power of attraction, of enjoyment, of joy.

And here's the key. That silent live air, that inner ahhhhhhh, turns out to be *the* most attractive thing there is. Lo and behold. As we just hang around in its vicinity by, say, resting our attention on a single breath, we notice, with growing clarity, just how naturally attractive that ahhhhhhh, that inner being, is. Then no one has to tell us to bear down and concentrate on soaking our mind in inner being any more than anyone has to tell us to bear down and concentrate on soaking our body in a hot tub. It just feels good. This is why I can tell the guy at the party that meditation doesn't take discipline. How much discipline does it take to eat a hot fudge sundae?

But don't the venerable old meditation texts talk about concentration as a key element of meditation? Yes, they do, but here's the thing, and it's one of the biggest misunderstandings in the whole field. Concentration—*natural* concentration—is a *state*, not an act. It's not something you do, it's something that happens to you. Again, back to nature: If you're smelling exquisite aromatic cedar, or fragrant roses, you don't have to make an effort to concentrate. If you're tasting a perfect avocado, your mind doesn't do a lot of wandering. If someone's giving you a great massage, or touching you in an erotically pleasurable way, no one has to tell you to pay attention; all by itself, your attention becomes naturally concentrated on that enjoyable experience. That's one of the reasons why Tibetan spiritual art is chock-full of images of happily copulating, enlightened couples: the pleasure they're enjoying is a demonstration of how natural concentration works.

~

We're going to move on now to several additional types of meditation. You can think of them as different *vehicles*. They all get you to the same destination, but depending on where you're coming from on a given day—what kind of terrain or weather you'll be driving through—it may make more sense to take the Jeep or the Prius, the dirt bike or the skateboard. Eventually you may find that, in general, one or the other has become your go-to vehicle. And just as you might favor the Mustang when you're younger and the Chrysler later on, you may find that this or that technique is more suited to you at different points in your meditative life.

What these vehicles all have in common is that they're natural, so they're easy riding and simple to drive. They're all versions of methods that have been used for centuries, so they've been thoroughly test-driven by our predecessors as well as by yours truly. They're vouched for . . . certified pre-owned. All is well.

Happy motoring!

5. Meditating on Sensation

Now let's explore another meditative technique. As before, first please read through the instructions in a relaxed way, lightly imagining yourself doing the meditation, then put the book aside and practice. Don't worry about doing it right—whatever happens is fine. Afterward, read the instructions again.

Sit comfortably, close the eyes, loosen up the body, and let things naturally settle.

Let everything be as it is, including the breath. This time we won't give the breath any special attention.

After a little while, notice your experience of hearing. You may notice the sound of an airplane, passing traffic, music, voices, air-conditioning or heating or the hum of the fridge—whatever. Sometimes there may be comparative silence, but even that has a subtle texture, what recording engineers call "room tone," and that also is heard.

See if you can predict the next sound you'll hear. . . .

Nope, didn't see that car horn (or dog bark, or whatever) coming.

See if you can *control* what will be the next sound you hear. . . .

Nope again.

So hearing keeps changing—unpredictably, uncontrollably—from moment to moment. There's nothing to do but remain naturally open to hearing and go along for the ride, casually noticing whatever we notice.

Whatever's there, just rest aware.

There's nothing special going on: it is what it is. All that's different is that, for once, we're resting in it, not trying to change things, acknowledging that we *can't* change things, gratefully giving up.

As before, when thoughts are there, they're just there. Don't try to block the thoughts, or clear the mind, or concentrate on anything in particular, not even the hearing—just lightly pay attention to it. When the attention drifts elsewhere, gently bring it back. Actually, you never have to come "back" anywhere, as hearing is always right *here*—within the "I," the experiencing awareness we always are.

Remain like this, easily resting in hearing, till you feel it's time to come out.

~

In later sessions, you can expand this practice to the other senses. Start as above. Then casually notice your experience of seeing. Even with the eyes closed, some subtle, shifting dance of color and light goes on. As with hearing, don't try to do anything about it. Just rest in the sense of seeing, and let it be however it is. Hearing may move to the background of your attention, or there may be a more integrated sense of resting in hearing and seeing together. Either way is fine; go with what's easy and natural.

At some point, notice the sense of feeling: the weight of your body in the seat, the temperature of the air, the clothing against your skin, the more internal sense of tightness or looseness here and there in the body. You can rest in that, with the other senses either in the background or sharing the foreground, however they present themselves.

Notice the sense of tasting and then the sense of smell. They may be there very subtly, like room tone.

Don't feel like a circus juggler, ever vigilant, hustling to keep all five balls in the air. Just passively rest in each moment of the spontaneous, ever-changing, unpredictable, uncontrollable dance of sensation. In any given moment, it doesn't matter which sense may dance to the front of the stage or what each sense might present. The content is immaterial. The resting, the inhabiting of the dance, is all that matters.

Whatever's there, just rest aware.

Whatever's there, just rest aware.

Whatever.

Just rest.

Naturally, thoughts will come and go. They're also part of the dance; there's nothing special about them. In fact, notice that thinking is actually another sense. Each ripple or wave of thinking has a sort of subtle texture or flavor, as it were, that's different from others. Their content doesn't matter either.

Remain like this for as long as you like, then take plenty of time to come out slowly.

6. Fine Print (Outer)

One day Moses goes up to the mountaintop, and God tells him, "Moses, remember the Sabbath day and keep it holy."

Moses replies, "You mean one day a week we should think about you and all the wonderful things you've done for us?"

God speaks a bit more slowly and deliberately, emphasizing his words, as if Moses hasn't been paying attention. "Moses: Remember . . . the Sabbath day. And keep it . . . holy."

Moses says, "Oh, you mean on Saturdays we shouldn't do any work?"

God, now clearly annoyed, speaks even slower. "*Moses! Remember! The! Sabbath day! And keep! It! Holy!*"

Moses says, "Wait a minute. You mean from sundown Friday till sundown Saturday we shouldn't drive cars or use machines?"

Now completely exasperated, God barks, "Moses . . . just do what you want!"

I learned that joke from a rabbi, one who likes people to find what works for them rather than worry about doing things "the right way." As you settle into your meditative life, I hope you'll do it in that spirit. For example: Now that you've been introduced to a few different techniques, which one will you practice? That's up to you. Sometimes you may want to do one, sometimes another. Or after a few sessions you may feel that one particular method is calling you, at least for now. Some people feel a strong affinity for breath-based meditation; some feel more free and open without the breath as a vehicle. And we're going to explore several additional methods, so there's still plenty to discover about what works for you. The important thing is to continue to take a little time to practice each day.

And really, this whole book is about just *one* method: naturalness, the way of noneffort, resting aware. *How* you drive is more important than *what* you drive. Person A, resting the attention effortlessly on the breath, has more in common with Person B, resting the attention effortlessly on sensations, than with Person C, straining to concentrate on the breath. That principle will apply to *all* the methods we explore together. It ain't what you do, it's the way that you do it. So just take it easy, let it all unfold on its own, and whatever you do will be fine.

But is it really that simple? There has to be some fine print, doesn't there?

Well, there certainly might be areas where you have questions, so let's address them, mainly to get them crossed off your list. As we do so, please keep in mind the big picture: the simplicity that we experienced in just paying relaxed, nonchalant attention to the I-sense, or a single breath, or the dance of the senses. Don't take anything in this book as a cue to make that simplicity complicated, in the name of "improving" or "helping" your meditation. I can still hear my father, with his well-practiced Brooklyn aggravation, imploring my mother, "Amelia, you wanna help? *Don't help!*"

∾

For now, let's focus on the outer aspects of meditation. We'll get to the inner aspects a couple of chapters from now.

Where should I meditate?

Anywhere—on the bus, on the train, on the beach, on your favorite deck chair, on your bed, on your fire escape, on your La-Z-Boy. When I'm in New York, I love practicing on a good, loud subway car. Sure, if there's a comfy corner in your home or a tranquil spot in your garden where you like to sit, that's great. But real tranquillity is an inside job. It's important to know that you don't have to wait to get to your special spot, that you can find your silent core anywhere.

It's especially good to discover that you can find it in the workplace. Since a meditation can consist of a single conscious breath, you can do that under the radar, if necessary, right at your desk, and you'll probably find that several such microsessions a day can very effectively keep workday stress from building up. With a little creativity, you can probably find a place to do longer sessions: if you don't have a cubicle you can use, perhaps there's an empty conference room, or a nearby park bench or church that's available during a coffee or lunch break.

Ten or fifteen years ago, you might have been justified in keeping your meditation in the closet so your colleagues and management wouldn't peg you as a weirdo or a slacker. But by now it's gone so mainstream that in most workplaces it's regarded as a plus. Many corporations (especially, for example, in the tech field) actively encourage their workers to meditate, sometimes even bringing in instructors, knowing that the result will be greater creativity, productivity, and harmony.

How often should I meditate?

If you can make meditation a part of your daily routine, like brushing your teeth, that's great. Brushing your teeth doesn't take a lot of discipline. It makes you feel better, so you do it, probably at least once a day.

Take a person who spends twenty-four hours of every day *engaged* in stuff: laughing at the jokes, avoiding the disasters, trying to figure things out, thinking about the past or the future, wondering when he'll get a break if there's too much going on, looking for a magazine if there's too little. In other words, a typical, normal person. Now imagine the same person spending twenty-three hours and fifty-nine minutes a day engaged in stuff, and one minute letting it all go. There's a world of difference between the two. And everyone has a minute.

Last year a couple I know had a hot tub installed in a corner of their garden, beneath the loquat trees—one of those pretty, round wine-barrel-style ones. They love soaking under the stars in the cool night air, or early in the morning as the sun comes up. At first they called the dealer a few times to ask how often to add chlorine, check the pH level, clean the filter, and change the water. One thing they didn't have to ask was how often to get in. How often should you soak in the healing, easeful inner waters of meditation?

It's a good thing, you like it, you do it. As it happens, my friends use their tub almost every day. And when they don't, they really enjoy getting back to it the next time.

When is the best time to sit?

When you'll actually do it.

If there's a particular time that fits into your usual schedule, it can bring a sort of graceful rhythm to your day. In India, it's said that the ideal time is in the hour or two before sunrise, and certainly there's a quiet vibrancy in the air then that you can almost taste. But some people are night owls, and pre-sunrise is just not gonna happen. That includes me. When I *do* get up, I shower and stretch a little; then it feels very natural to pull up a cushion and sit. For others, the most natural time of the morning might be during a coffee break, or between classes, or on the bus or train during the morning commute (but not while driving . . . or operating heavy machinery).

Sitting in the morning does tend to put you in a nice, open, clear space that can help set you up to move smoothly through your day. On the other hand, evening practice (perhaps on the train home, or in your bedroom or garden when you arrive, or with your partner before supper) can be a lovely way to decompress from the day. Or you can sit both morning and evening.

Some people find that sitting up in bed and meditating just before slipping off to sleep puts a nice end to the day and helps them sleep more soundly. Others find that it makes them too energized to sleep. And some find that practicing just after a heavy meal makes meditation feel sleepy and dull. These things are pretty individual; you can experiment with finding the times that suit you best.

While it's good to have a regular practice time, don't feel limited by it. All sorts of formerly "dead" times can be brought to life. One great discovery is that you never have to wait again. Anytime you're in a waiting room, instead of automatically reaching for *People* or *Sports Illustrated*, you can close your eyes and turn the place into a being room.

Don't put off meditation when you feel stressed or upset or otherwise "not in the mood." That's backward. If you wait till you're in the mood, you could wait forever. Conversely, don't reserve meditation for the times you feel bad, like an aspirin you take when headache strikes. Practicing with some regularity, irrespective of passing moods, is how, for centuries, people have transformed their lives—by tuning in to that which is deeper than passing moods.

How long should I sit?

Well, let's see. How long should you hold hands with the one you love? How long should you walk in the park, or sing that catchy tune? In all these cases, we don't bother about the time, so we don't much notice it. Sit for . . . a while.

Some people set themselves up carefully on their chair or cushion, with their wristwatch at the ready or their clock conveniently in view. They dutifully rack up the fifteen or thirty or forty-five minutes that they or someone else has prescribed for them, and completely miss the present. That's called "doing time," and it's a self-constructed cell, the opposite of natural freedom.

One of the watershed moments in my own explorations came when I threw the clock out of the room. There's a saying that there's no time like the present, but actually there's no time *but* the present—we've already seen this by meditating on a single breath. One moment of letting things be, not worrying about the time, marinating in timelessness, is far more beneficial than forty-five minutes of doing time. And then, if you happen to continue marinating for a while, that's fine. Sometimes less is more; and then, if you're in a nice groove, sometimes more is more.

Of course, for practical reasons, you may need some clocklike device to make sure you leave for school or work on time, but in that case it's best to use a timer so you can set it and forget it. I would use a smartphone alarm and choose a quiet, gentle tone. When your nervous system is settled in meditation, an alarm that seemed fine before might sound harsh or jarring.

One thing that *doesn't* work well is "Hurry up and relax"—rushing to get to your cushion on time so you can cram in your full dose. Occasionally when I'm leading a public session, someone will come bursting through the door with that unmistakable wild-eyed, out-of-breath, late-for-class look. Then they spend the whole session trying to settle down. Really, they'd be much better off taking their time and then coolly slipping into the room a few minutes late.

Is there such a thing as overdoing it?

Soaking three times as long in the hot tub is not necessarily three times as good. Most people will intuit the right balance between silence and activity, but a few may feel drawn to meditate for hours a day. Extended practice can, in fact, help instigate some very rapid unfolding of consciousness, but that's best done on a retreat with an experienced guide—more on that later. If you just meditate all day and stop taking care of business, you'll probably generate chaos that'll be no fun for anyone. (On the other hand, you may well recognize some hamster-wheeling that you can happily drop out of.)

There *are* times when it's good to meditate as much as possible. One is when you're ill or recovering from an injury or surgery. The meditative state is highly conducive to accelerated healing and helps maintain a peaceful, settled mental state in the face of medical problems. When my first wife underwent several months of cancer treatment, she meditated through most of her chemo. The doctors and nurses were so impressed by her grace under fire that they brought her back to teach the whole staff to meditate.

It's also great to meditate more during pregnancy, increasing your sitting time as you get closer to term. Some research has indicated a correlation between lower maternal stress and decreased risk of miscarriage or of long-term effects on the child such as hyperactivity. Meditation may also help smooth out the effects of hormonal changes such as mood swings, both during pregnancy and postpartum. One of my earliest teachers, when asked about the effect of the mother's meditation on the fetus, put things in less clinical terms: "Swimming in bliss!" Some women report being able to dip in and out of meditation during labor and even report that it makes delivery quicker and easier.

At the other end of the life cycle, knowing how to let go into meditation can be a great relief when it's time to let go into dying.

Whether you're looking at weeks in hospice or a few last seconds after being hit by a truck, meditation can help you make a conscious, peaceful, graceful, perhaps even blissful exit. (Of course, that's the final exam. Hopefully you'll have plenty of time to prepare before you take it.) If it's someone else who's dying, you can discreetly radiate tranquillity and vibrant silence just by quietly sitting beside the bed or in a corner of the room. This can help maintain a space of clarity and OK-ness for the dying person, as well as for harried medical personnel and distraught relatives.

Is meditation contraindicated for some people? What about those suffering from mental illness?

People whose emotional stability is shaky should generally start with modest doses of a few minutes a day, just to be cautious. Once it's clear that they're OK with that, they can slowly increase the time if they wish.

If you're under the care of a physician or mental health professional, by all means follow their advice. More and more of them are learning ways to effectively integrate meditative practice with other forms of therapy. In general, meditation in reasonable amounts supports mental and physical health. Almost every week a new study shows that meditation may ease ADHD, or emotional anxiety among students taking tests, or physical manifestations of stress among professional athletes. But it's not a panacea. In cases of clinical depression or schizophrenia, for example, extended sitting may not be advisable. Serious mental illness requires professional attention, possibly including medication.

What about my sitting position? Do I need to sit cross-legged on a cushion?

First, let's take a step back. Is it essential that we sit to practice? Why is that the default position, so to speak?

The nervous system associates standing with the busy waking state: active and alert. It associates lying down with sleep: passive and inert. That leaves sitting as the Goldilocks position, just right for *passive alertness*, aka meditation. But if you're one of the many people who can meditate lying on your back without routinely falling asleep, feel free. In fact (in a story we'll get to later), one of the most revered sages of the twentieth century, Sri Ramana Maharshi, attained enlightenment in that position.

Otherwise, sit. How? However you'll be comfortable enough and at ease enough that you'll enjoy doing it and *keep* doing it. I suspect that many of the meditation dropouts are those who tried to mimic the perfect posture—to look like the guys in the books—and then, reasonably enough, started "not getting around" to their next session of self-inflicted torture. But just in case you feel inclined to tune up your posture beyond the La-Z-Boy position, there are some time-tested options.

The Thinker

Let's consider two great works of art. You can see them both in Paris, about a mile apart—fittingly, on opposite sides of the Seine. First, in the garden of the Musée Rodin, is *The Thinker*. Rodin originally called it *The Poet*, but his astute foundry workers renamed it: they recognized the intensity with which this body hurls itself into thought. It's beautiful, of course, but it sits in an inherently unstable pose, with chin propped precariously on the back of the hand, elbow propped even more precariously on the knee, and back uncomfortably bent. The whole body

The Seated Scribe

leans forward, its center of gravity somewhere over the knees. This is the body—and mind—of one who is not content where he is, but feels compelled to thrust himself ever onward into a future of new developments, new situations . . . new thoughts. When you want to generate a lot of intense thought, sit like *The Thinker*.

At the Louvre you can see *The Seated Scribe*, a painted limestone Egyptian sculpture from the time of the pyramids. He's sitting *up* by sitting slightly *back*, with his weight squarely over the base of his spine. It's a pose of effortless, natural balance—he looks like he could sit there all day. Body and mind are fine right where they are. His eyes show that he's vividly awake, receptive, ready to receive whatever comes next, without judgment, as fresh and open as the blank papyrus in his lap. When you're the Pharaoh's scribe, you'd better be wide-awake, ready for whatever he dictates, not full of opinions about it. This is a posture conducive to passive alertness. When you want to meditate, sit like this.

Easy Pose

Half Lotus Pose

Three words: Sit. Back. Comfortably.

You can do this in your chair, no problem. Gently slide the base of your spine snug against the back of the chair. Have your feet square in front of you on the floor; if your legs are short, put a cushion under your feet so they don't dangle. Rather than crossing your arms, which maintains some tension, rest your hands naturally on your lap or knees. If you're on a bed or couch, you'll probably want to put a pillow or two behind the small of your back, and you can cross your legs beneath you if that's comfortable.

If you want to declare your independence from furniture, you may find that there *is* something that feels good about sitting with your back not pressing against anything: free, in open space. Depending on how you're built and how flexible you are, you can try the Easy Pose—essentially like the scribe's—or the Half Lotus Pose.

In both of these poses, you can rest your hands either with palms up in your lap, one on top of the other, or with palms down on your knees, which is favored in some Tibetan teachings (and which I find the most natural). If your knee sticks unphotogenically up in the air, don't try to force it down; gravity and your growing flexibility will bring it down naturally in due time. Whenever your ankles get achy or your legs get stiff, you can gently straighten and stretch them. The Full Lotus Pose is strictly for those who've been doing a lot of yoga or are very young and flexible.

Full Lotus Pose

These poses usually work best if you use something to raise your hips higher than your ankles. This moves your center of gravity up and back, centering your spine over your hips and making it easy to sit upright, even for long periods. The traditional *zafu*—a round cushion about fourteen inches across and seven inches high, usually stuffed with kapok, a plant fiber—is perfect, but you can also use a couple of cushions from your couch or ordinary pillows. Before you sit

Cow-Face Pose

on a *zafu*, fluff up the kapok by squishing the rim in toward the center. Otherwise it gets flat and hard—rookie mistake!

Some people find that the Cow-Face Pose is the most comfortable, and that it doesn't require a cushion. Others prefer the Seiza Pose, which derives from Japanese culture and which you may have seen in martial arts classes. It's especially effective at keeping

Seiza Pose

the back straight without effort. The traditional no-cushion version is tough on the knees, but you can solve that by stacking two or three cushions under your butt.

Once you're settled in position, you can close your eyes and gently rock left and right a few times, like a metronome, gradually allowing the rocking to diminish as you find your center of gravity along the left-right axis. Then do the same along the forward-backward axis: you may notice that your natural center of gravity is a little farther back than you might have thought.

Or you can forget all this and just flop into the Hammock Pose, in which I've personally logged many of my most sublime meditative interludes. ("Moses . . . just do what you want!")

Hammock Pose

Again, don't focus on trying to look like the people in the books, including this book. No one—not Buddha, not Saint Peter, not Simon Cowell—is sitting in judgment and deciding, "Yes, perfect posture, we have a winner, this one gets through the pearly gates of nirvana," or, "Nope, slam the gate shut on this schlump." That judge you hear in your mind is just . . . your mind. Real, authentic, natural posture comes from the inside. It's like acting: one of the worst things an actor can do is to rehearse in front of a mirror, focusing on the outer expression rather than the inner experience. Don't try to sit like a Buddha—just sit. That's how a Buddha sits.

Here's an inner approach to posture I learned from my wonderful teacher of meditative singing, Gina Salá:

Sit in your preferred position, but deliberately let your spine and head slump forward. Close your eyes and feel the earth beneath you—the solidity with which it supports you and the fertility with which it gives rise to all life. (The earth is always there beneath you, and if you pay attention you can always feel it, no matter how much furniture or infrastructure is between you and it.) Now feel a just-risen sun start to glow in the sky above you and warm the earth. As the earth grows warmer, a tiny seed at the base of your spine begins to sprout and sink its roots deep into the earth. Slowly, slowly, it unfurls and grows toward the sun, naturally unfurling your spine, from the bottom up, till the sprout grows through the roof of your mouth to the top of your skull. Now you can feel your spine and head in their natural, balanced, easeful position. You'll know this is right posture, not because it looks "correct" from the outside, but because it feels *good* from the inside.

As you continue your practice and become more at home

with this inner sense of posture, you can reconnect with it occasionally as you go through your day, whether you're driving or working or standing at the grocery checkout. It will feel good all over again and reconnect you with the ease of the meditative space, even in the midst of activity.

Is there a best way to go into your practice, or do you just sit down and do it?

Sometimes you may want to take a few moments to loosen up or decompress first. Particularly if you've been very caught up in busyness, it might not be that helpful to plop down on your seat, snap your eyes closed, and go right on being busy in your meditation. A simple way to emerge out of that busyness is, after sitting down, to just easily look around the space you're in: Look over there. Hmmm. And there. Hmmm. And over there, across the room. Hmmm. Not looking to find or see anything in particular. Just lightly, casually looking about, with no agenda . . . and then, at some point, letting the eyes close and continuing—agendaless.

There are also the simple methods of physical loosening that we mentioned earlier: neck rolls, trunk twists to left and right, shrugging the shoulders up toward the ears and then dropping them, or anything else that feels good. You can also draw in a slow, deliberate, extra-deep breath through your nose, hold it for a few moments, then open the mouth and release the breath with a big, loud sigh—like the sigh of relief when you come home after taking your last test on the last day of school, toss your book bag into a corner, and flop onto the bed. You might want to do a few of those.

This sigh of relief is not just a matter of imagination. The breath is deeply connected to our neurological functioning and thus to our states of consciousness. (If you ever, for some obscure reason, want to precipitate a nervous breakdown, try breathing rapidly in and out through your mouth.) Yogis have explored this deep connection extensively for centuries, and have devised consciousness-optimizing breathing exercises called *pranayama*—the word roughly rhymes with *Dalai Lama* and literally means "breath extension." Here are two forms of pranayama that are great pre-meditation settler-downers. (**Caution:** If you have a condition such as asthma, emphysema, or hypertension, consult your physician before practicing pranayama. Never force the breath or the retention of the breath in any way. If you feel dizzy or light-headed, stop immediately.)

Ujjayi (OO-jahy) breath is very simple. (The name literally means "victorious," but in yoga classes it's often called "ocean breath.") Get settled in your sitting posture. Breathing normally through the nose, slightly constrict your throat, much as you do when you're whispering or fogging up your glasses to clean them, so that, as the breath goes in and out, it makes a quiet rasping or ocean-roar sound (or Darth Vader sound!). This slight constriction slows down the breath, makes it more conscious and deliberate, and converges the senses of hearing and feeling upon it.

Nadi shodhana (NAH-dee sho-DHAH-na) is a bit more complex, but after you've done it once or twice it will feel quite natural. (The name means "channel clearing," but you may hear it called "alternate-nostril breathing.") First, check that the flow of breath through both of your nostrils is reasonably clear. If, say,

Right Nostril Closed

Left Nostril Closed

the right nostril is blocked, lie down on your left side for a few minutes, till they equalize. If both are very blocked, put this off for another day and just do ujjayi breathing.

Now, get set in your preferred sitting position.

Leaving your left hand in your lap or on your knee, bring your right hand up to your face. Breathe in normally through the nose. Throughout this exercise, it's preferable to use the same throat constriction as in ujjayi breath.

Now put your right thumb on the right side of your nose, close your right nostril, and breathe *out* through your left nostril. Then breathe *in* through the left nostril.

Next, close the left nostril with the third and fourth fingers of your right hand as you open the right nostril by taking your thumb off it. Breathe *out* through the right nostril, then *in*.

Then once again switch nostrils by closing the right nostril with the thumb and releasing the left nostril.

Start the cycle over again and continue in this way. What it comes down to is *breathe out, breathe in, switch nostrils. Out, in, switch. Out, in, switch.* As you're doing this, you may tend to tense your right shoulder or lift your right elbow; keep them dropped in a relaxed position. Finish on a left-nostril out-breath, let your right hand drop to your lap or knee, and easily slip into meditation.

With either of these two breathing exercises, as you continue you'll probably notice that it feels very good, very satisfying, to let the breath become naturally fuller, deeper, and slower, and to let the pause at the end of the inhale and the pause at the end of the exhale naturally lengthen. On the inhale, you can have the idea of expanding your ribs out 360 degrees toward the horizon, like the slats of an expanding barrel, filling your lungs to capacity with fresh, new air. At the end of the exhale, you can contract your abs to squeeze out the last bit of stale, old air. Everything should be full, but nothing should ever be forced.

You may notice that the pause at the end of the out-breath and the pause at the end of the in-breath are silent. You may also notice that the breath is invisible. So you're pouring the invisible into the silent. Just go on for as long as you like . . . pouring the invisible into the silent.

I used to have a girlfriend who would read the *New York Times* while doing pranayama. Clearly, if you're reading (or texting, or watching TV), you're missing the point. This is a very powerful method for leading the mind, body, breath, and senses to harmonize and settle down together. It can be a lifesaver for someone having a panic attack or a bad drug experience. According to the traditional texts, it also revitalizes various subtle internal energies in healthful, rejuvenating ways. As with everything else, give it a fair trial and see what your experience is. But I'll bet money that, after a few minutes of pranayama—no matter what you were doing or how you were feeling before—you'll feel extremely settled and centered, your jets thoroughly cooled.

Speaking of cool, I keep getting chilly halfway through the session.

This happens to many people as their bodies settle down in meditation. You might want to have a sweater close by or wrap yourself in a shawl.

What if my nose itches?

Ah . . . to scratch or not to scratch? Some venerable traditions insist firmly—even adamantly—that you not scratch the itch (or stretch the aching back, or blow the runny nose, or extend the numb leg). But in the view of other, equally venerable traditions, making a project of sitting stone still, just to earn the merit badge for motionlessness, is more of a distraction than a simple scratch would be. My old teacher Maharishi used to say, "Better five seconds of scratching than five minutes of itching." And years after my brief exposure to no-motion Zen, I was delighted to fall in with Tibetan teachers, who, while sitting in meditation, will scratch, stretch, or even help themselves to a drink of water. It's just no big deal. It's only natural.

Why is it so important to come out slowly at the end?

Both the mind and the body can become very deeply settled in meditation. Because this settling process is natural and gradual, we often don't realize just how settled we are. This is one reason why it's fruitless to try to evaluate your meditation while it's going on. Sometimes you might be thinking, "This is a waste of time, I'm just sitting here," and then your phone rings or someone calls your name, and you realize, "No, I really don't want to come out right now."

To come out of this deep state quickly could be jarring, and could result in a spacey feeling or even a headache. So it's good to take as much time as you feel you need, or in any case at least a minute or two. Some people need quite a bit more time to ease the body from the settled state back into the active state. Stretch, twist, rub your face or hands, and so forth, and eventually crack your eyes open slowly. If you have the time, sometimes you might even want to lie down for a bit.

This slow reentry can be a rich experience in and of itself (a real eye-opener, so to speak). I remember once teaching a young woman in New Orleans. After her first session she seemed quite amazed at something—speechless, really. Finally she said, "I don't think I ever opened my eyes slowly before. I never realized that I can see my own eyelids!"

How about meditating with music?

There's lots of traditional understanding of how specific sounds, including some music, can help lead the attention into silence. We'll learn about them in a later chapter. But in general, it's best not to depend on music or anything else. I've been fortunate to have this lesson driven home in my work with inmates, some of whom have been put into "administrative segregation" (solitary confinement) for weeks or months at a time, with no TV or radio. When they come out, they say things like, "It was a struggle at first, but eventually I realized I could make it a retreat. I found out I don't need anything. Everything else was taken away, and I found out what can't be taken away."

You've mentioned hot tubs a few times as a metaphor for meditation. How about actually, literally, meditating in a hot tub? Or a sauna? Or while getting a massage?

The short answer is, why not? Meditate everywhere. If you're in a situation that's already relaxing, why not go deeper into it with some spontaneous meditative settling down? On the other hand we can say, as with the question about music, don't become dependent on it. Since you can meditate anywhere, sure, do it on the massage table; but since you can meditate anywhere, also do it in the dentist's chair. (Guy asks his priest, "Father, is it OK to smoke while I pray?" "Certainly not!" "Well then, is it OK to pray while I smoke?")

The Bhagavad Gita, one of India's most esteemed texts on the various enlightenment paths, has a few verses about selecting a place to meditate, recommending that the seat be "not too high and not too low." Perhaps we can extrapolate from this advice to a general sense of moderation. When choosing a place to sit—if you have a choice—avoid, say, the extreme heat of the sauna and the extreme cold of the ski run. But ultimately, know that you're fine where you are. Wherever you be, you can Be.

7. Meditating on the Heart Center

The heart is not just a blood pump.

It includes a system of about forty thousand neurons, which some researchers call the "heart brain" or "little brain." It sends information that affects cognition and perception to the head brain, it emits an electromagnetic field that extends several feet from the body in all directions and is far stronger than the brain's, and there are indications that it can form memories and generate feelings on its own.

Centuries before science started tracking these matters, cultures and languages throughout the world formed a consensus that, when we speak of the heart, we mean more than the physical organ. We can also mean the essence of something, the "heart of the matter," or a person's sense of his own essence: "At heart, I'm an artist." We can mean both the seat of our emotions—"My heart is full"—and our sense of empathy: "Have a heart." When children attest to the truth, they cross their hearts. When we've learned something so thoroughly that we can take the thinking mind out of the loop, we know it by heart; when we buck up our confidence, we take heart. And this confluence of meanings is not unique to English. In French, for example, *coeur* has most of the same connotations—and is in turn related to English words like *cardiac*, *courage*, and *core*.

Art and religion are full of images that represent the heart as the core of love and devotion in their purest, most enlightened forms, whether it's Jesus pulling back his cloak to reveal the Sacred Heart radiating light beams of omnidirectional love, or the monkey god Hanuman clawing open his chest to show his beloved Rama-Sita eternally abiding there, or diamond-hearted Mahavira, or the Care Bears, or all those valentines we got in grade school. Perhaps Superman's pectoral S-shield suggests that the heart is the seat of our true superpowers. Spiritual guides, from Saint Augustine in the fourth–fifth centuries to Sri Ramana Maharshi in the twentieth, have taught that the heart is the meeting-place where humans can commune with the Infinite.

Some Eastern traditions speak of vortexes called *chakras* (literally "wheels"), located throughout the body, that manifest various forms of life energy such as sexual desire, creativity, or spiritual insight. In that system as in the West, the heart center is associated with love. Certainly *something* seems to be going on in that area besides blood circulation. When we're heartbroken or have a heavy heart, we *feel* something there.

And in certain moments when we've been overpowered by some kind of higher feeling that takes us beyond the usual smallness of self, we may feel as if the heart is brimming or bursting open, almost as if the self itself has momentarily burst open. It might happen when you melt into love with another person, or watch a poignant film, or experience a sublime work of art or music. I can remember, in the weeks following the 9/11 attacks, hearing stories of the firefighters who ran into the buildings as everyone else was running out. I repeatedly had that bursting-chest feeling and burst into tears—not so much in grief as in awe, as if their sacrifice of their own lives to something larger somehow pointed *me* to something larger, in the face of which I could only burst open.

All this is just some background, some context for the heart meditation we're about to explore, in case this kind of talk resonates with you. If not, that's fine. This method is a favorite of mine, and of many of my students. In my experience, it can be intensely effective in helping to open the heart—whatever that might mean—and keep it open. But don't take my word for it. Again, as the Buddha said, "Believe that which you have tested for yourselves." As usual, we'll walk through the process step by step, with no belief or attitude required. As usual, please check your expectations at the door. We're not looking or striving for any particular feeling or experience.

∼

As before, sit back comfortably in your preferred position and close the eyes.

Do whatever physical or mental preparation you feel at home with, such as twisting and loosening up the body, finding your internal posture, perhaps doing some pranayama.

Then just sit easily for a minute or so, breathing normally, letting things be as they are.

Now, easily bring your attention to a place deep in the center of your chest.

As the breath continues to flow naturally in and out, imagine that it's flowing directly in and out of this place, deep in the center of your chest, the heart center: flowing in from all directions and flowing out in all directions, 360 degrees.

Don't try to do anything special with the breath, just let it go however it goes. Let the breath take care of itself as you easily rest your attention in the heart center.

After a while you may feel inclined to forget about the breath entirely, or the breath on its own may settle down till it's barely perceptible. Fine. Just rest your attention in the heart center.

Let the experience of the heart center unfold on its own, however it unfolds. Don't try to give the heart center a size or shape or boundary. Just remain easy, open, attentive.

At times, you may feel subtle sensations in the heart center, such as a warmth or tingle or hum or vibration, or something too subtle to name. Or you may not. However it is, it's perfect. In each moment let it be as it is, and then let it be as it is in the next moment. Whatever's there, just rest aware.

At times, it may feel as if the heart center becomes very small, even microscopic, or it may seem very big, as if it has expanded to the walls of the room and beyond. You may feel as if *you* become large or small with it. Or you may not. Perfect.

Thoughts and sounds, sensations and feelings may come and go as usual within the awareness. As usual just let them come and go, paying them no special mind as you rest in the heart center.

Sometimes the heart center may seem to be experienced as some kind of light—perhaps very subtle, perhaps vivid. If so or if not, fine; just be with it however it is. The light may seem to spread, radiate, permeate, engulf. You may even feel that everything, yourself included, is melting into that light. However it is, just be with it—not judging, not resisting, not favoring, just along for the ride.

Remain like this for as long as you like. Then take plenty of time coming out.

8. Fine Print (Inner)

Chapter 6 dealt with the outward, physical aspects of meditation. Now let's take up questions that may arise about the more inward, experiential aspects.

The physical preparations for meditation, such as posture and pranayama, are helpful. Is there some kind of recommended inner preparation—some mental adjustment?

That depends on you. If there's someone who, for you, embodies ultimate wisdom and kindness, whether it's Jesus, the Dalai Lama, Amma-ji, your granny, or Hello Kitty, you might like to have their picture where you're going to sit. Just gazing at it can remind you of What's What, and ease your way into slipping into the zone of What's What.

Many traditions start with some kind of invocation or setting of intention. In Mahayana Buddhism, a session typically begins with the reminder that we're practicing to help bring true happiness and freedom not just to ourselves but to all sentient beings, from our dearest loved ones to our worst enemies, from the worms beneath our feet to the unknown beings in unknown worlds. If you feel drawn to it, you might want to pause for a moment and dwell on some such thought.

I like the advice that the great Cuban jazz trumpeter Arturo Sandoval once offered to musicians:

Every time we have the opportunity to sit down and practice, . . . take three seconds only. Three seconds. . . . Look up and say, "Thank God." . . . Because you're so grateful, you're so glad, that instead of doing something else you're about to start practicing, which you have to take as a gift from God, because you don't have the necessity to be breaking stones in the mine, or driving a truck from Oklahoma to Key West, or something like that. You're sitting down with your beloved instrument— practicing!

Of course, if you're more comfortable thanking life or the universe than God, that's fine. The point is that it's a fortunate few who encounter this knowledge of how to luxuriantly settle down within yourself, *and* have the ears to hear it, *and* have the leisure to put it into practice. In Tibet, the Chinese government has banned pictures of the Dalai Lama, the exiled spiritual leader. I've met monks who keep photos of him hidden in their temples. Late at night, after their Chinese guards have gone to bed, they take them out and meditate with them, risking prison and torture. It's good to appreciate the preciousness of your situation. Thank your lucky stars.

One more bit of musician's wisdom that can help set the right attitude comes from a 1964 Chuck Berry song: "No Particular

Place to Go." There's no particular state to achieve, no particular feeling to have, no particular way for your meditation to proceed. Each moment is however it is. Wherever we are, we're always right *here*, not on our way to somewhere else. In Chuck's words, we're just "Cruisin' and playin' the radio / With no particular place to go."

This recalls the saying among some religious people that, when you pray, you should assume that your prayer is already answered. Assume that the meditation is already accomplished. It *is* already accomplished, because it's a matter of just being, not doing, and you already *are*. Look down at whatever piece of furniture you're sitting or lying on right now. How hard do you have to work to be on that chair? That's how hard to work at being in meditation. Don't worry about getting it right—it's already right.

I keep falling asleep in meditation.

You're under arrest.

No, actually you're normal. This happens to most people now and then. As with scratching the itch, there are indeed traditions that take a less natural approach, insisting that you tie yourself to the mast and resist sleep at all costs. The other view is that sleep is a natural and healing experience. Better five minutes of sleeping than twenty minutes of fighting it (nodding out, then shaking it off, like guilty, sheepish parents at a school concert). If sleep comes occasionally, we can presume that the body, in its wisdom, is taking what it needs. But if sleep comes regularly, consider whether you're encouraging it by sitting in a less-than-alert posture or practicing right after heavy meals or too late in the day.

It can also be a matter of avoidance: the mind is dipping its toe into the pool of transcendence and saying, "It's too cold." Don't fall for it—the water's fine.

I can't find a quiet place to meditate.
Excellent. Perfect.

But the noise is so distracting.
Actually, it isn't. Your quest for silence is distracting.

Please consider two places where I've frequently led sessions:

1. A cozy meditation center, converted from a graceful Craftsman-style home, under a couple of palm trees in Santa Monica, a few blocks from the beach and the sidewalk cafés of Main Street. An affluent, older couple often attends. As soon as we finish and open our eyes, they both invariably start complaining about the occasional buses that run past the place, "ruining the experience."

2. The bleak cinderblock chapel of a maximum-security prison in Newark, New Jersey. A huge loudspeaker hangs directly above our heads. About half a dozen times per session, bone-rattlingly loud announcements come over the speaker and ricochet against the bare walls: "ATTENTION ALL AREAS, ATTENTION ALL UNITS: SPANISH CHOIR OUT TO THE GYM. SPANISH CHOIR OUT TO THE GYM." My inmate students continue to sit, unfazed. No one complains.

We live in a noisy world. If you set yourself the task of shushing it, your work will never be done. Fortunately, noise is no problem. Noise is just . . . noise. Actually, it's just *sound*. When we call it "noise," we're already subtly judging it, labeling it as an annoyance, as something that shouldn't be there.

What do the prisoners have going for them that the complaining couple doesn't? It's not a superpower of "blocking out" sound. You will never, ever succeed in blocking out sound, I assure you. The prisoners live on tiers where there's a nonstop cacophony of radios, TVs, raucous conversations, heated arguments. They don't have the luxury of picking out this sound or that sound and trying to wish it away. They've been forced to learn that *it doesn't matter*. All you have to do about the sound is not engage with it.

It's good to learn about this not-engaging early on. Years ago, one of my very first teachers came to Berkeley to teach meditation. His local students gave him a tour of the rambling Victorian house where the instruction would take place, and then asked him which room he wanted to use. "Which room is the noisiest?" he replied.

Actually, though, you've always known how not to engage with sound. You do it all the time. You can be in a restaurant with conversations, music, and clinking cutlery all around you, yet none of it prevents you from enjoying the conversation at your own table. You don't think about "focusing" or "concentrating" on your conversation; it's all much simpler and more natural than that. True, you might sometimes find yourself dining next to people who never learned to use their inside voices, or who forget after the third bottle of wine; and then, if possible, you might discreetly move to another table. Similarly, if you're meditating, say, on the train, and you find yourself close up with people cheerfully shouting into their cell phones, there's nothing wrong with changing your seat, or even slipping on a pair of earplugs or noise-canceling headphones. But it's best not to depend on them. Give yourself a chance to discover, like those inmates, that it finally doesn't matter what's going on around you. Your inner peace and OK-ness don't depend on your getting the outside world to cooperate with your plans.

I have so many thoughts.

Or: *I have too many thoughts.*

Or: *I can't stop thinking.*

Or: *I can't block out the thoughts.*

Or: *My thoughts are about big, disturbing issues.*

Or: *My thoughts are about annoying, trivial issues.*

Or: *All I seem to do is sit there and think.*

Et cetera.

We'll have a whole chapter on this topic later on—not because thinking is a problem, but because people *think* thinking is a problem. But for now, here's the short version:

Thoughts are exactly like sounds—only on the other side, the *inside*, of your skull bone. It doesn't matter what the thoughts are about. It doesn't matter whether they're few or numerous. *Thoughts are just thoughts*, just mental sounds, which you've defined as mental noise. (That definition is also a thought.) Just as you'll never, ever succeed in blocking out the sounds, you'll never, ever succeed in blocking out the thoughts. No one does: not the Buddha, not the Dalai Lama, not the Zen or yoga teacher who looks so peaceful. What they *have* succeeded in doing is giving up trying: they've succeeded in noticing that *thoughts don't matter*.

Remember, this is *natural* meditation. Just as it's natural for the ear to hear sounds and the eye to see forms and colors, it's natural for the mind to experience thoughts. They're just part of the texture, the landscape, the wallpaper, the background against which you're paying attention to the heart center or whatever you're meditating on. As we'll see in Chapter 9, thinking is actually another sense. It's some motion within the sensing-I, like currents within an ocean. The ocean remains undisturbed.

Anytime you notice that your attention has gone away from (say) the heart center and on to some train of thoughts, that's fine. That happens to everyone. It's part of the process. Just as naturally and matter-of-factly as your attention shifted away from the heart, now shift back to it. Don't try to stick it with some extra oomph ("This time I'm gonna *stay* here"). Don't try to shove away the thought ("And don't darken my doorstep again"). That kind of trying just gets you more tangled up. Trying to push away the thoughts—or the sounds, or anything else—is a backhanded way of engaging with them, and that gives them power. Ignore them, just as you expertly ignore the people at the other tables in the restaurant. They're none of your business.

Sometimes during meditation my sense of my own body changes. Out of the blue, I start to feel heavy, or light, or bigger, or smaller. What's going on?

These sensations are fairly common. At other times you might feel tingly or floaty. Sometimes you might feel like your hands have disappeared, or your head or the space between your eyebrows has become huge.

All of this is fine and none of it particularly matters. You're starting to settle into the core of your being, which is beyond time and space. Something whose spatial dimensions previously seemed very set and solid, like your body, now starts to soften up.

So the dimension of time could be softening up too?

Yep.

And that's why sometimes I have no idea whether I've been sitting for five minutes or two hours?

Yep.

I just get bored and restless. I thought this was supposed to be pleasant and "attractive" to the mind.

Sometimes, despite all the guidance toward natural, effortless sitting, people fall into effort. That's completely understandable. In most of our endeavors, whether it's building a business or learning to play the piano, the results are directly proportional to the effort: sweat equity pays off. Meditation is the one activity (or, rather, nonactivity) where the results are *inversely* proportional to the effort: less is more. It goes against the grain of almost everything we've done, and, deep down in our bones, we can find it hard to believe that easy really does it.

That's fine. You'll try as much as you need to try till you're convinced that trying doesn't work. It's self-defeating, it *prevents* settling down, and that's going to make meditation tedious. Most people go through a certain amount of this. It's clearly recorded that the Buddha did, and that his enlightenment came when he finally stopped trying. You try for a while, then just laugh at yourself, give up, stop trying to *do* meditation, and let it do you. Again, *Gompa ma yin, kompa yin.* "Meditation isn't, acclimation is." There's no meditation process to do, but there's a process of acclimating to the fact that there's no process.

You've probably gone through a similar acclimation process in your work or sport or relationship. You gradually or suddenly realize that you've been hustling to cram more data into those spreadsheets than is needed, or you've been gripping the racquet too tightly, or working way harder than necessary to explain your feelings to your partner when you can just relax, look into his eyes, and let him see where you're coming from. Just leave a bit of room for naturalness, and it creeps in . . . naturally. Try a little tenderness.

Imagine that you're passing a lazy afternoon at a sidewalk café on a mild spring day, sipping your drink, chatting with a couple of friends, and watching the cars go by. That's easy. In fact, it's effortless: the cars just go wherever they go, and you're happily unemployed. But now suppose that for some reason you suddenly fall under the delusion that you're a traffic cop. You jump up, try to direct traffic . . . and everyone ignores you. That's going to be frustrating and tedious.

Good news—you're no cop. Sit back down, sip your drink, and relax.

Sometimes I find weird moods coming up. I get agitated, or even angry.

There's a sort of emotional discharge that can take place in meditation, a neurological clearing-out process. It's like flushing your radiator—all kinds of rust and crud can come out, and that's a good thing. What's *not* helpful is trying to analyze or interpret it: "Oh, I'm angry because of *y*," or, "I'm sad or afraid because of *z*." The emotional energies that arise don't necessarily correlate with what's going on in your life—they may represent a clearing-out of junk you've been unconsciously carrying around for years—but it's all too easy to *connect* them with what's going on. Don't take those false connections seriously. In particular, never jump up out of meditation to *act* on them. If you've ever dreamed you were yelling at your ex, then woke up ready to grab the phone and continue the argument, you know what I'm talking about. It would be funny if you were watching it happen in a Ben Stiller film.

But suppressing that discharge (or, rather, *trying* to suppress it) is another bad idea: putting a lid on a boiling pot only increases the pressure. So what to do? What's the third way?

The clue is that the other word for emotions is *feelings*. We call them that because they *feel* a certain way. A feeling is not just an idea, such as "My friend dissed me, therefore I'm pissed," or "Meditation is pointless: I'm sitting here with nothing to do, therefore I'm agitated." (Sometimes there's nothing to do yet we feel perfectly content.) Feelings are sensations somewhere in the body. Happiness *feels* a certain way—maybe a sort of effervescence in the chest or a lightness around the skull. Anxiety might feel like butterflies in the stomach and itching in the palms. Depression might feel like a dull weight pressing down on the top of your head.

If anxiety, anger, or any other feeling comes along and is just some mild atmosphere in the background of your experience, don't worry about it. But if it's so strong that it stomps up to the foreground and demands to be addressed, note how it *feels* . . . physically. Neutrally, nonjudgmentally, matter-of-factly, allow yourself to experience the sensations—in your chest or the pit of your stomach or wherever they are—without trying to suppress or amplify or interpret them. Any thoughts that accompany them should be lovingly disregarded like any other thoughts.

The key here is that sensations are *just* sensations. They're just there, like different kinds of weather, independent of any emotional subtext or overlay. By simply *observing* the sensation, without getting embroiled in a dubious narrative, we allow it to be whatever it is and to play out in its own good time. The weather blows over.

The lesson here, which you can actually apply to *anything* that happens in meditation, is: Just say "Hmmm." There's a scene in *The Big Sleep* where Humphrey Bogart, as the detective Philip Marlowe, is considering a clue. Tugging at his earlobe, he says, "Hmmm." When Lauren Bacall asks him, "What does 'Hmmm' mean?," Bogey replies, "It means, 'Hmmm.'"

That's all. Having many thoughts or few thoughts? Hmmm. Falling asleep or feeling superalert? Hmmm. Feeling that you're attaining enlightenment or wasting your time? Just say "Hmmm."

Sometimes I find that a muscle or limb unexpectedly twitches, or I even sort of jump in the chair. What's going on?

This is another form of neurological discharge, well known in the annals of the various meditative traditions, and completely benign. Ngak'chang Rinpoche, a Buddhist lama I used to study with, gave the example of a rubber band that's been tightly wound up. If you put it on a tabletop and let it go, it will dance and twitch erratically as it unwinds itself. That rubber band is our nervous system, and through the letting-go of meditation we're all unwinding. In some people it takes the form of physical movement; in others it doesn't. Either way, it's no big deal. Hmmm.

Sometimes I see subtle inner colors or kaleidoscopic patterns.

That's another not-uncommon, not-important experience, especially when you're meditating on sensing. And sometimes these inner sensations are not so subtle but quite flashy. In addition to visual phenomena you may feel inner textures or hear inner sounds such as buzzing or humming, or even taste flavors or smell aromas—all possible symptoms of settling down into more rarefied levels of sense perception. Subjectively they can be very pleasant, but don't try to hold on to them, or to get back to them when (inevitably) they go away in the ever-changing flux of experience. They're also just part of the passing landscape.

I've always thought of meditation as requiring effort. Now you keep emphasizing effortlessness, and I find myself trying not to try. Help!

Good point. Let's not fetishize effortlessness; let's not make goal-lessness our new goal. I promise, the meditation police won't come and arrest you for trying *or* for not trying. But when you feel frustratingly caught up in trying, or trying not to try, or trying not to try not to try . . . just drop the whole thing. Take a deep breath, let it go with a loud, long, 360-degree sigh, and just remain in the space that the sigh carves out. Or else, fine, *make* effort, till you get good and tired of it. In fact, make more effort, make supreme effort, so you get a chance to see, once and for all, whether that works.

More experienced meditators I've met have told me that to really meditate I need to concentrate, or stop my thoughts, or sit in a particular position, or breathe a certain way, or count my breaths, or . . .

Sometimes it's important to nod and smile and ignore what people say—or at least understand where they're coming from when they say it. Assume that their intentions are good and thank them graciously. Also remember that people like to be *right*. They like to know that whatever they're using is the *best*, whether it's a mobile phone or a meditation technique. And sometimes misery loves company. There are hundreds of forms of meditation, and many of them do involve effortful concentration—or, at least, instructions that people may *interpret* as requiring effortful concentration.

For that matter, there are traditions that say to meditate properly you have to sit on a black cushion, or you have to sit on a maroon cushion, or you have to learn Sanskrit and study texts for three years or seven years before you can even begin to meditate. I say, be a good scientist. See what your own, actual experience is, and don't let other people talk you out of it.

What's the best meditation? Well, what's the best camera? There's a saying that the best camera is the one you have with you. A cousin of mine who's an excellent photographer owns a fancy, expensive DSLR with a big honking zoom lens. It takes great pictures—in theory. In practice, it doesn't take any pictures at all, because it's too big for her to schlep around. She winds up taking most of her pictures with her iPhone, the camera for the rest of us, and they look fine. The best meditation is the one you'll actually *do*, that you can carry into your real life.

If someone tells you that you have to silence your thoughts, you might ask them to do the math and calculate how many total hours they've spent trying to do so . . . and out of all that, for how many total seconds they've succeeded. That should end the conversation quickly.

Some people claim they can achieve the same effects by taking psychedelic drugs. Am I wasting my time with meditation when I can just drop some acid?

There's a long history of the use of psychedelics as sacramental agents to experience heightened states of consciousness. And the great rise in interest in meditation and inner development in the West took place in the sixties, just as psychedelics started flooding into the counterculture and trickling into the mainstream. People have been asking this question ever since. Now, fifty years later, we're in a better position to respond.

Of the present generation of senior teachers of meditation, yoga, Buddhism, etc., lots of us did some pretty serious tripping back then. Many will credit psychedelic substances with first opening their eyes to the cosmic dimension. But I don't know any who will flatly state, "It's the same thing," or advise their students to run out and take acid or mushrooms. Lots of people have had spectacular, short-lived experiences; no one, to my knowledge, claims that *any* substance has produced a stabilized state of enlightenment.

Perhaps psychedelics are—at best—like a movie trailer. Is the trailer "the same" as the movie? Yes and no. It may present the same plot and evoke the same tone, but it's compressed in a way that can be misleading. It can serve the legitimate purpose of whetting your appetite for the actual film, but it omits the subtle nuances and the long story arc, emphasizing instead the most intense, flashiest moments, and hyping the whole thing by brightening the colors and cranking up the volume. In all that intensity, the movie's true themes may easily be lost. You can wind up confused.

How do I know meditation is working? Sometimes I feel like I'm just sitting there and nothing's happening.

We *can't* evaluate what's going on while it's going on. Meditation consists of resting the attention in some object of experience, such as the breath, and remaining neutral and nonengaged with whatever's going on. When we try to judge or evaluate the meditation, we give up our neutrality and become engaged. It's like scowling into a mirror while you complain about the lines on your face . . . which are caused by scowling.

Also, because the subjective experience is so, well, subjective, it's an unreliable measure of what's going on objectively. A friend of mine was one of the key researchers in some of the pioneering studies on the effects of meditation. By studying changes in such functions as brain waves, oxygen consumption, and galvanic skin resistance, he helped establish the physiological reality of the meditative state. At the end of a session, as he was taking the electrodes off a subject's scalp, the subject would often say something like, "Ah! That was a nice, deep, silent meditation. I'm glad you got that one on the record," or, "Oh, that was one of those shallow, choppy meditations. All I did was think thoughts. I hope this one doesn't throw off your averages." To my friend's surprise, once he examined the results he found that, physiologically, both subjects had undergone a similar degree of settling down. You just can't tell.

That is, you can't tell *during* practice. The point of meditation is not just to have some pleasant experience during meditation, then come back to the same-old same-old. The real effects are experienced during the other twenty-three and a half hours of the day.

When Ed Koch was mayor of New York, he was famous for riding the subways, walking around town, and asking people, "How'm I doin'?" That might be a great way to run a city, but it's not a great way to meditate. We're in the middle of a process, like water flowing toward the ocean. If the water keeps asking itself "How'm I doin'?" it's likely to come up with answers like, "Not so good; you're hitting rocks; they don't feel like ocean," or, "Still winding through this valley—no ocean in sight." The water *can't* know how it's doin', and even if it could, what use would it make of this information? "How'm I doin'?" is a thought. As with any thought, don't try to suppress it, but disregard it. Like any thought that's repeatedly disregarded, it eventually loses its power.

But I had this great, blissful meditation the other day, and now I can't get back to that peaceful place. What am I doing wrong?

Nothing—except trying to get back somewhere.

Remember that you're just passively along for the ride—the scenery will be constantly changing, and it's none of your business. Again, it's a *natural* process, and nature is change. What's going on in your body, mind, and environment constantly changes, from digestion and quality of sleep to your commute time and the proximity of tax day. Also, the process of emotional discharge of old neurological junk is ever changing and unpredictable. As a result, your nervous system and the way it experiences everything—including meditation—are also constantly changing.

Your memories of previous meditation experiences, whether "good" or "bad," can become a whole new set of expectations to unexpect. Don't buy into them; just know that they're also thoughts to be disregarded.

After a while, I'm not sure that I'm doing the specific technique anymore, but I do seem to be settled into some nice, peaceful place where I don't feel the need to do anything—where it would somehow be too much to go back to paying attention to the breath or the heart center.

Excellent. Remember, these techniques are vehicles. What you're saying is that you've arrived; then it's completely appropriate to step out of the vehicle, hang out, and enjoy. If at some point you start to feel unarrived again, you can get back into the vehicle.

This seems like a lot of fine print to remember.

It's not really a matter of remembering a bunch of material, like studying for a test. It all ultimately points to the same thing: the simplicity of natural practice. Once you get the feel of that, you can forget about the rest. It's sort of like learning to drive. At first you may keep mentally running through everything you learned in Drivers Ed: "Release the brake, ease on the gas, signal, head check to the next lane . . ." After a while, you just drive.

So just sit. Especially by sitting every day, you'll quickly see how simple it is. Use this chapter as a reference for as long as it's useful, and then consider it to have been written in disappearing ink. Just take it easy and enjoy being. Whatever happens is fine.

9. Meditating on Sound

I have a brother-in-law who's a bit of a wise guy. I love him dearly, I know he'd walk through fire for any member of the family . . . *and* he's a bit of a wise guy. Also, he's a gifted comic actor, with a Belushi build and a huge, booming voice. Whenever there's some mention of a meditation workshop I'm going to lead, or a meditation retreat my wife and I are going to attend, or anything else meditation related, Peter spreads his arms wide, turns up his palms, joins the tips of his thumbs and index fingers, clamps his eyes shut, screws up his face, and bellows, "OMMM-MMMMM!!!!!"

I laugh along with him. I get a kick out of the guy. But I also quietly relish the irony of the situation. Even in the act of making fun, even in spite of himself, he winds up participating in a centuries-old meditative practice. Sure, on the thinking level of the mind—the upstairs level—he's enjoying it as parody, but down in the echoey basement of consciousness he's still generating that powerful sound, and it's resonating throughout his being. Help yourself, *compadre*!

Not only wise-guy brothers-in-law, but every third-grader in the world seems to know *Om*. Mention meditation to a group of eight-year-olds, and they'll all go into the same slapstick routine. Even when it's acted out on this cartoony level, there's something about the idea of meditative sound that seems to spark a universal response. And now that you've experienced meditatively melting into such objects as the breath, the senses, and the heart center, the idea of meditatively melting into a sound might not seem so wacky. In a few moments, we'll look at some ways to do that.

You probably know that, in some traditions, these sounds are called *mantra*. Nowadays, news media use the term to mean any oft-repeated slogan, like the 2008 Republican battle cry, "Drill, baby, drill," or the Obama foreign policy, "Don't do stupid stuff." But rather than pound on one idea like a slogan, a true mantra helps us go beyond our ideas. It bypasses the conceptual mind through its sonic qualities, a combination of soothing and enlivening effects that promote the state of passive alertness. Either mantras have no dictionary meaning or their meaning quickly dissolves into pure sound . . . and then the sound dissolves into pure awareness.

But we've *all* engaged in meaningless sounds, often joyfully. Throughout the world, kids chant happy, repetitive nonsense songs and pass them on to the next generation of kids. And the Latin, Hebrew, or Sanskrit verses that many people hear or intone in their worship may work best when they're not understood.

Years ago, I was on a plane from Texas to New Jersey, coming home from a retreat with my friend Jodi. I'd been going through some intense emotional turbulence, and she gave me a teaching that's one of the most profound I've ever received. "Dean," she said, "just remember this. No matter what's happening, as long as you say *Wheeeeeee!* you can't have a bad time." Try it. Seriously. It may be all the mantra you'll ever need.

What does *Wheeeeeee!* mean? What does *Hey Diddle Diddle* mean? Or *Zip-a-Dee-Doo-Dah*? Or *Rama Lama Ding Dong, Sh-Boom, Sha Na Na, Ob-La-Di Ob-La-Da, Gabba Gabba Hey, Boola Boola, Hey Ya, MMMBop*? It's a secret no one knows. Yet each sound has, we could say, a different flavor, a different texture. Some dictionary words have a soothing, mellow, sonorous, mellifluous sound: *undulate, swallow, chimes, chrysanthemum, antebellum, marveling, manatee, boron, lozenge, ardent, rhino* . . . and, for that matter, *soothing, mellow, sonorous, mellifluous*. Great poets like Coleridge know all about these words and use their power to evoke worlds of imagination:

> In Xanadu did Kubla Khan
> A stately pleasure-dome decree:
> Where Alph, the sacred river, ran
> Through caverns measureless to man
> Down to a sunless sea.

Like superconcentrated poetry, mantras are words of power. They're resonant vibrations that have been test-driven for thousands of years by yogis and sages who are finely tuned to the subtlest levels of consciousness, and who have confirmed these mantras to be ideal vehicles, like submarines for diving beneath the conceptual level into our own unshakable, deepest identity—delicious, pure beingness.

A mantra can instantly reawaken your connection to this deepest level. That can be especially useful when you're on a battlefield or otherwise in the thick of things. Most of the guys I've worked with in prison have made that discovery. When a guard has you facedown in a puddle or a belligerent fellow inmate is trying to bait you into a fight, invoking your favorite mantra can quickly restore your big-picture perspective. Of course, for the mantra to be right there when you need it, you have to have practiced with it—you have to do the fire drill before the fire. Here the great example is Mahatma Gandhi. When the assassin's bullets tore into him, it is said, he was chanting the name of *Ram* before he hit the ground.

My friend Jeremy once asked me, "Why do you repeat these mantras so many times?" That question has many answers. One is that words that touch on our highest impulses—like "I love you"—bear a lot of repetition. Another is that actually there's *no* repetition in mantra practice. As we saw in the meditation on a single breath (and as I hope you're continuing to see in all your meditating—and in all your living), it's always right now, this moment. In right now there's no time for repetition. We can never say the mantra more than one time, *this* time. Whenever the practice seems repetitious, that's the feedback mechanism alerting you that you've gotten caught up in the illusion of time again. The cure is more "repetition," not less. Keep repeating the mantra till it leads your attention back to nowness and you see that nothing is repeated.

Another answer to Jeremy's question is that most of us, for most of our lives, have been silently repeating something we could call "antimantras," usually on a subliminal level—unexamined formulas that *have* meaning, often toxic meaning, and that gain hypnotic force through their repetition: "I'm not loved," "I'm not OK," "I deserve less," "I deserve more," "Everything happens to me," "I have to fix everything," "If my loved ones ever die, it will be an infinite catastrophe."

One popular strategy for thwarting all that negative autosuggestion is positive autosuggestion, but that gets us into dicey territory, like Al

Franken's sappy Stuart Smalley character on *Saturday Night Live*: "I'm good enough, I'm smart enough, and doggone it, people like me!" We laughed at Stuart in his powder-blue cardigan, cooing affirmations into his mirror, not only because his approach was so saccharine but because it was feeble. It's just pitting thought against thought, mind against itself. We need to go deeper than thought, to get down into the basement and rattle the house.

Thus, traditional wisdom offers a more effective strategy: invoke the resonant power of thought-free mantra, use it to carve out some space and time in which *no* thoughts control the field, free ourselves from their spell, and see clearly What's What. Fortunately, What's What is delicious, and doesn't need to be spiced up with the artificial flavors of cheesy affirmations. I once asked Ngak'chang Rinpoche why we were learning to perform a particularly elaborate, mantra-heavy Tibetan ritual. He responded, "Because while you're doing this, you're not doing anything else." It keeps you—and your mind—off the street.

~

As we've said before, it ain't what you do, it's the way that you do it. There are plenty of people in various traditions carefully counting out their *Hare Krishna*'s or *Hail Mary*'s or *Om Mani Padme Hung*'s on their beads, and working hard at accumulating enough repetitions to earn some kind of spiritual merit badge. I've tried that, and, as far as I can see, it's the beans-in-a-pot approach. Fill up the pot with mantras, and then you've got something.... Yeah, you've got a pot of beans.

But if you use mantra in an open, easygoing, timeless, nonstriving way, the results will be golden. A mantra that lends itself beautifully to this kind of practice—one that you've been using all your life—is *ahhh-hhhh*, the sound of openness. Anatomically, it's the sound you produce when your vocal apparatus is in its most wide-open condition. It's a completely natural, deeply human sound, uttered spontaneously by people of all languages and cultures to express the open states of surprise, revelation, letting go, and contentment—including the kind of perfect-moment contentment we imagined at the beginning of this book. As a result, it's used extensively in at least one formal spiritual system, Tibetan Buddhism. The lamas have thoroughly test-driven and approved it. Personally, I've put a lot of mileage on this vehicle, and I recommend it enthusiastically.

To meditate with the mantra, you can start by sitting in your preferred position.

Close your eyes and loosen up a bit as desired.

Take a nice, full breath, appreciating the way your ribs expand and the pressure of the breath massages and stimulates your insides.

Then open the mouth and sound out a prolonged *ahhhhhhh*.

Then take another breath and do it again.

And again.

Continue for as long as you like.

Pay relaxed attention.

See what happens.

Perhaps the most important point is that we don't *push* out the sound but effortlessly release it. Think of yourself as a balloon. If there's any effort at all, it's in the filling of the balloon, the in-breath. The mantra sounds on the out-breath, which is pure letting go. On a deeper level, as my singing teacher Gina Salá advised me, always *hear* the mantra first, already resonating in the silence. Tune in to it, then just allow it to come through you. This way, you're not working to produce the sound. You're a conduit.

At some point, you may feel inclined to sound the mantra in a quieter way, subvocalizing it under the breath. That may feel more inward, more settled. If so, go with it. Just keep letting the attention easily ride the mantra, and don't mind whatever else (thoughts, sensations, and so forth) might be in the background.

At some point, you may feel inclined to leave off even subvocalizing and just entertain the mantra mentally. On this level, the mantra tends to stop being distinct repetitions, running together into one continuous ahhhhhhhhhhhhhhhhhhhhhhhhhhhhhhhhhhhhhhhhhhhhhhhhhhhhhhhhh . . . with no beginning or end. You may notice that you don't have to exert any effort to generate the mantra mentally. Again, it's already there, always there, and you can just tune in and listen to it at will. Your experience of the mantra may at times settle into some extremely subtle inner hum or vibration. However it goes, just keep listening to it, settling into it, soaking in it, without judgment, without goal.

At some point, even this very subtle mental experience of the mantra may melt away, the way a cough drop melts in your mouth. Then it has served its purpose. Don't hold on to it, but let it melt, leaving . . . whatever it leaves: silence, spaciousness, passive alertness, I-awareness. Remain like that for as long as you naturally remain. Then, if you find yourself coming back up to less silent, less settled levels of experience, you can pick up the mantra again, not distinctly but on a comfortably faint, subtle level, and then take another dive. Stay with this process for as long as you like, then come out slowly.

~

You can do this meditation on *ahhhhhhh* very fruitfully and enjoyably for a lifetime, just like this, and find the experience getting deeper, clearer, and more spacious. Most important, you'll find this spaciousness seeping more and more vividly into your experience of daily life. But if you're interested, there are some additional directions in which you can take mantra practice.

Finding Your Sa

If you like using mantra aloud, you might want to find the optimal pitch in which to intone it. Just sounding it somewhere in a range that feels comfortable is perfectly fine. But in case you feel motivated to fine-tune it (literally), then you can use what musicians in India call your *sa* (pronounced "sah")—that is, your natural key. First, experiment by singing low notes till you find the lowest one that you can barely sing; if you try to go any lower, it becomes a barely audible croak or a tuneless breath. Locate this lowest note on a keyboard, and from there count up seven or eight half-steps, each black or white key being a half-step. That brings you to your sa, the tone where your particular anatomical structure optimally resonates, producing the fullest, most open sound with the least effort. For most men, the sa is somewhere around C or C-sharp, plus or minus one or two half-steps; for most women, it's around G-sharp or A. (And everyone's voice is lower in the morning.)

Another direction of exploration is to try other mantras. For the kind of sitting practice described above, *bija-mantra*, so-called seed sounds of one or two syllables, are considered most suitable. Om is not just a punch line for third-graders and brothers-in-law. In some traditions it's considered *the* cosmic sound, embodying in vibrational form the essence and totality of existence, and it has proven its potency in the practice of dedicated meditators for centuries.

> When Siddhartha listened attentively to this river, to the song of a thousand voices; when he did not listen to the sorrow or laughter, when he did not bind his soul to any one particular voice and absorb it in his Self, but heard them all, the whole, the unity; then the great song of a thousand voices consisted of one word: Om—perfection.
>
> —HERMANN HESSE, *Siddhartha*

> Om! Om is the imperishable word. Om is this universe. . . . Om is all that is past, present, or future. And whatever is beyond the bounds of time is also Om.
>
> —MANDUKYA UPANISHAD

Ironically, despite its fame Om is commonly mispronounced. The second letter, usually printed as *m* in our alphabet, is not actually *m*. There *is* a letter *m* in Sanskrit, but this is not it. It's actually something called the *anusvara*, or "following sound," a nasalization; you can hear it in the French *bon*, *soupçon*, or *croissant*. Although you do lightly close your mouth, unlike the true *m*, the anusvara is not produced by bringing the lips together. This is not just a matter of linguistic nit-picking. If you sit quietly, close your eyes, and experiment, you'll find that *o*-plus-*m* vibrates in your lips and ends there. *O*-plus-anusvara vibrates in your whole head, your whole body, your whole consciousness, and its dissolving-into-silence helps *you* dissolve into the silence of just being.

You may also feel drawn to chanting or reciting longer mantras, the very same *Hare Krishna*'s or *Hail Mary*'s or *Om Mani Padme Hung*'s I may have sounded like I was pooh-poohing a few pages back. Not at all. I was merely taking issue with the *way* people often use them, mechanically racking up their totals. Jesus also took issue with that, condemning "vain repetition." If it's experienced as repetition—that is, if it's experienced as something we're cranking out in time—then indeed it's in vain. But now we've been steeped in pure nowness, simple beingness, through our various meditative methods, including the method of riding one syllable all the way down to the bottom of our being. Having done that for a while, now we can chant or recite our rosary and find that same power there.

Some people are attracted to practices in which longer mantras are sung melodically, often in a group. These are found in many traditions, including Indian *kirtan*, which generally uses a call-and-response style. In recent years it has grown more popular in the West, where kirtan tracks are often played in the background of yoga classes. The best-known American kirtan *wallah* is Krishna Das, whose soulful, chesty baritone comes from a place of deep devotion. There are other superb singers as well. My favorites include Jai Uttal (an innovative world musician and sort of a passionate Roy Orbison tenor to Krishna Das's Elvis), Wah! (devotional techno-goddess with a Fender bass), and Gina Salá (sunrise in a bottle). Just listening to their recordings or singing the mantras on your own may be powerfully opening for you. (Jai Uttal's album with Ben Leinbach *Music for Yoga and Other Joys* is near the top of my desert island playlist.)

You may feel motivated to go further and participate in live kirtan, which in recent years has become widely accessible in concerts and festivals. Unlike the quiet, solitary practice of sitting with eyes closed and melting into a mantra, group kirtan can seriously rock, with people playing instruments, clapping, and dancing: it's been called "the gospel music of India." The richness of Indian culture has produced literally thousands of mantric names for the Ultimate. That's the sort of thing that in some parts of the world has led to holy wars, but kirtanistas are generally having way too much fun rocking out to argue about which name to sing. As Krishna Das has said, "You can call it anything—but call it!"

It might not seem obvious how such a practice can lead us into the space of just being, but it can. Like sonorous words, music has power of its own, and can deeply influence our consciousness. The sound of bagpipes can stir people to cry, march into battle, or (so I've heard) lose control of their bladders. And finding the expansive meditative space in such an active, communal context can move us toward seeing that it's not only inside us, but everywhere. As Jesus says in the Gospel of Thomas, "The kingdom of heaven is inside you and also outside you."

In kirtan, much depends on the song leaders. It's crucial that they connect with the practice at a deeper level than mere performance or emotionality. The best ones may be fine musicians, but they completely offer up their musicianship in service to that deeper connection, and their singing somehow invites you into that connected space rather than leaving you outside, as an audience to a performance. American kirtan often mixes traditional Indian elements with aspects of gospel, rock, blues, or even hip-hop. (Check out MC Yogi, who raps joyous tunes like "Ganesh Is Fresh" and "Rock On, Hanuman.")

Some purists object, but I suspect that that kind of cultural adaptation is not only OK but necessary. Whenever an inner technology is transplanted—as when Buddhist practice migrated from India to Tibet or Christian worship came to the Native Americans of the Southwest—it makes itself accessible by assimilating elements of the local indigenous culture. We Westerners grew up having our most poignant feelings invoked by the I-IV-V chord progression that runs from Bach to pop. We respond to that. In my own kirtan practice, I've done things like borrow the melody of "Red Red Wine"—a song that, for me, summons up all the heartbreak in the world—to sing *Om Namah Shivaya*, the mantra in which heartbreak and everything else dissolves.

On the purist side, there's also a less well-known form of meditative Indian music called *dhrupad*, whose roots go back through centuries of royal court musicians to the ancient temple singers. Classical dhrupad features a solo singer who starts with a long, low, slow, arhythmic, deeply contemplative improvisation that can make you feel like you're watching God pick up each element of the periodic table, turn it in his hand, and consider its possibilities. Then the *pakhawaj* drum comes in, things turn lively, and God sets the universe into joyous motion. You can't sing along with dhrupad, but you'll hear the human voice touch places you didn't know were there to be touched. The recordings of the virtuoso Uday Bhawalkar and Pandit Ritwik Sanyal are highly recommended.

There are many traditions that use the voice to invoke the transcendent spirit: Greek Orthodox liturgical music, Gregorian chant, gospel, Qawwali (passionate Sufi love songs to God—check out the recordings of the astonishing Nusrat Fateh Ali Khan), the Afro-Brazilian *pontos* of Umbanda, Tibetan mantra (including the multiphonic chanting of the Gyuto Monks, in which a single voice sings three notes simultaneously), and others. And it's not limited to so-called sacred music. Listen to the great proto–folk rocker Fred Neil in "The Dolphins" or "The Other Side of This Life." When his voice drops into that low third, it's like falling weightlessly into the basement under all the basements: complete and unconditional relaxation, total release of tension. *That's* letting go; *that's* how you meditate.

~

You can also forget about mantras and kirtan, and meditate on whatever sound comes along—what we could call *found sound*.

As I'm writing this on my deck, gusty winds are whipping through the region. Behind me, they're stirring the leaves of the trees with a sizzling sound, and to my right they play on the wind chimes. The boom of a jet fades into the distance. Occasionally I stop writing, look up at the sky or close my eyes, and just let the sound carry me along. Along to where? To nowhere. To now here. No meaning, no goal, no strategy, no problem. Just *wsssshhhhhh . . .* I got your mantra right here.

It's that simple. Of course, you can do this with the sound of your local stream, or the crackling of your fireplace, or the surf or the birds.

Everything is vibration, a passel of tuning forks, with which we can harmonize and attune. The nine-hundred-plus species of crickets all have unique mating chirps, produced by the serrated "teeth" on the bottoms of their wings: the Southern ground cricket, for example, advertises his machismo in F-natural. The universe itself, say astrophysicists, vibrates in B-flat, fifty-seven octaves below middle C, the deepest note that exists or *can* exist. Just trying to imagine that—playing a couple of descending octave-jumps on my keyboard and then trying to continue that series in my mind's ear—quickly blows my mind into a fine, scintillating silence.

If you live in the city and don't hear rivers or leaves out your window, you can listen to the rivers of traffic. If that challenges your assumption that automobile sounds are merely noise—an annoyance, something to tighten your defenses against while you wish you were in the country— well, good. You may discover that there's something liberating about opening to a sound to which you've been closed. If you doubt that the sounds of the city can be more than noise, Exhibit A is Thelonious Monk. He used to roam the streets of New York, listening to the cars and subways, banging a bent Coke can against brick walls and iron fences, then come home to his piano and incorporate it all into his next composition.

In my hippie days, I crisscrossed the country in freight trains, happily ensconced in an empty boxcar as the cities and cornfields rolled by, lulled by the clackety-clack of the rails, my mind thoroughly pacified. I could understand how the hoboes I met could do this year in and year out: I saw them as a kind of monastic order, tuned to a metallic mantra of their own.

∽

By resting your attention on found sound in this easy, goalless way, there's something you may discover about your senses that's subtle, yet revolutionary in its implications. For this method of exploration, I'm indebted to Rupert Spira.

We're used to thinking of sound as something we experience "out there," in an environment beyond our skin. But in actuality, all we know of sound is hearing, and hearing happens "in here"—in our awareness. We don't hear the dog across the street. We experience our hearing of the sound of the barking of the dog, and that experience takes place within awareness. Right now you can close your eyes, pay attention to whatever hearing presents itself, and check whether that's true.

Once that's been confirmed, you can do it again, but this time also check whether you can find a distinct boundary between the hearing and the awareness that's aware of the hearing—the "I" that hears.

Take your time.

You'll probably notice that you can't find a clear boundary. There is only, we could say, I-hearing, hearing-awareness. Rest in that.

Now do the same with seeing. As in our earlier meditation on the senses, notice the internal experience of shifting light and color, but now also notice whether there's a clear boundary between the seeing and the I-awareness that sees. . . .

In the same way, explore the experiences of feeling, tasting, and smelling, and notice whether there are clear boundaries between them and the experiencer. . . .

No. There's just I-sensing, sensing-awareness.

Also notice your experience of thinking, with its subtle textures, and see if there's a distinct boundary between the thinking and the I that's aware of it. . . .

No, just as there's no clear boundary between the ripples and the lake.

So, what are we left with? I-awareness-thinking-sensing. Rest in that.

As you rest in that, notice that there's no such thing as an interruption or a distraction. What can we be distracted by? Anything we might call "distraction"—a phone ringing, a door slamming, a thought or feeling arising, the light suddenly shifting—is part of this sensing-thinking-awareness in which we're resting. It's all awareness. It's all meditation. What we once might have called "meditation"—trying to block out the barking of the dog—is the distraction.

After spending some time in this kind of exploration, you may notice that your relationship to things and people "out there" in the world is quietly shifting. There may be a growing sense of intimacy, as you see that they're all "in here," inseparable from the awareness that you are. You can lightly remain open to that intimacy as you go through your day. This doesn't mean you have to hug everyone.

Years ago, a friend of mine was in Rishikesh, in the foothills of the Himalayas, and he and some fellow Westerners managed to get an audience with the revered holy man Tat Wale Baba. One of them asked, "Why is the River Ganges sacred?" Baba replied, "Because it's inside you." The Westerner asked, "Why is Mount Meru sacred?" Baba replied, "Because it's inside you." It went on like that for a while.

I don't have words to convey what it means for something to be sacred. But by exploring this area of intimate nonseparation, you may start to see it for yourself.

10. First Glimmers

So . . . how's life?

Now that you've been meditating for a little while, let's sit back and take stock of the early signs of change that may be taking place—the first glimmers of the carryover from the chair or cushion into your actual life.

In one sense, this conversation is unnecessary. Because this is a natural process, the results are the results. You do your practice, the results percolate their way out, and, in their own good time, they infuse the various areas of your life without being analyzed or even identified. But still, it can be useful to point them out. Sometimes these first glimmers are subtle. Giving them some attention can help us appreciate them more fully and so encourage us to keep practicing. And to some degree we can encourage the changes by making room for them, cooperating with the process as we sense our life turning a corner and taking a fresh direction.

My main form of transportation around town is a Vespa motor scooter. (It's powder blue, and I call it My Little Pony. It's a macho thing.) Whenever I take a new passenger on the back, I explain that when we go around a corner and the bike leans into the turn, you cooperate with it. This applies to life as well as scooters: don't force the lean, but don't resist it either—just feel how the bike wants to lean, and go with it.

Leaning with the Vespa

It's important to be clear about this, because it can be a big point of confusion. People sometimes think that now that they're practicing meditation they're never supposed to—or never *allowed* to—be agitated. Sure, when you've had some deeply peaceful moments in the meditation chair, you want to feel deep peace all the time, and eventually you will. (More precisely, you'll recognize that you *are* deep peace.) As you return from the chair to your daily routine, you can help make room for that transformation: step back a little, look with a bit of a detached eye at your old, habitual ways of acting and reacting, and know that wherever you see a better way you have the freedom to adopt it. But if you force the issue, you can wind up like Frank Costanza on *Seinfeld*, trying to lower his blood pressure by yelling "Serenity now!" and raising it instead.

Back in college I had a friend named Kip. I ran into him a few weeks after he learned to meditate, and asked how it was going. He replied that he felt more relaxed, he was emotionally more stable, he was getting along better with his parents, and so forth. But he was a bit disappointed because he had read about people starting meditation and quitting smoking, and it hadn't happened. "So finally," he said, "I just quit by myself."

For a moment I just stared at him. Then I said, "Kip . . . that's it! That's the change! What did you expect—that the cigarettes would jump out of your pocket and into the trash?"

These days, there's a growing body of scientific documentation of such results as decreased smoking, lower blood pressure, and higher grade point average. You can always get the latest by Googling "meditation research," and I'm glad that's there. But I'm more interested in the subjective, human, everyday stories I've been seeing for years. For example, while studies have shown the breathing tube relaxing and expanding when asthmatics meditate, I've never seen anything on sinuses. But yesterday a friend with chronic allergies reported that his sinuses open up whenever he meditates—and now the effect is beginning to carry over into the day. "It's really good to breathe," he says.

Again, because it's a natural process, the unfolding of the results takes a different course, at a different pace, for different people. Your mileage *will* vary. But the cumulative experiences of millions of meditators over thousands of years give us a pretty clear picture of where it all ultimately leads. The adventures of all the little streams on their way to the ocean will display some variety, but the nature of the ocean is well established.

WHAT—ME WORRY?

One of the first effects of meditation that many people notice is that anxiety begins to just . . . evaporate. ("Hey, where'd it go?") Situations may remain the same, and responses to situations are still required, but somehow the whole thing has less static cling. You take care of business and you move on.

This can be a revolutionary development in our lives. Almost everyone around us habitually reinforces the notion that worry is a necessary, even inherent part of our grown-up functioning. TV commentators routinely ask experts questions like, "Do we need to worry about higher taxes next year?" Knowing zero about tax policy, I can answer that one right now with 100 percent certainty: No, you don't have to worry about higher taxes. Yes, you may have to *pay* higher taxes. No, worrying about your taxes won't lower them.

I once spotted a tongue-in-cheek bumper sticker on Route 22 in New Jersey: "*The more you worry, the longer you live.*" This vividly brings home to us how unproductive and just plain silly worrying is, yet we're exposed to such a constant stream of worried chatter that it's easy to get caught up in it. Meditation gives us a break from all that. Even if worried thoughts continue to buzz around our skulls as we sit, that's all right, as long as we continue to disregard them. In fact, that's a good thing; it's part of the process. Every time a worried thought knocks on your door, calling you to come out and play, and you ignore the call, that worry loses some of its power. Eventually it will stop bothering to come around. You just keep sitting and, over the days and months, worry gradually dissolves.

When you get up from your cushion or hammock, you can keep cooperating with that dissolution—leaning with the Vespa—just by having some insight into the futility of worry. You can watch *other* people worry and see whether it helps their problems or exacerbates them. And in your heart you can silently thank them for the lesson. Unwittingly, they've put themselves through that mill so that you don't have to.

As the sixth-century sage Shantideva taught:

If there's a solution to the problem, what's the point of worrying?
If there's no solution to the problem, what's the point of worrying?

PEACE, ENERGY, CLARITY

As worry evaporates, what's left in its place is a natural state of peace: we're more relaxed, centered, balanced, content. The effects of that peace can sneak up on you in subtle, unexpected ways. Maybe one day you notice that you've fallen out of the habit of automatically firing up the radio the moment you start your car—you don't need that constant outer noise to drown out your inner noise, because you don't *have* so much inner noise. Things just feel kinda quiet and comfy inside.

At first, you may notice this sense of calm and balance only in certain situations. One student of mine who was an avid golfer realized early on that he was less tense while putting: his hands were steadier and his scores improved. Over the next few months, the same calm gradually came to pervade his other activities, at work and at home. As he put it, "It's like my whole life became the putting green."

You may also notice that the nature of this new, enhanced relaxation defies the stereotype of the mellow meditator as a passive, apathetic slacker. Just ask the Bulls and the Lakers about the eleven NBA champi-

onships they won after Phil Jackson made meditation part of their training. An interviewer once told the great actor Peter Ustinov that he must
have nerves of steel to get up on stage to perform, say, *King Lear*, with its
four hours of passionate soliloquies. Ustinov replied, "I think steel is the
wrong analogy. I think it's extreme relaxation." Starting with our example of *The Seated Scribe*, we've seen that meditation is about being in
repose but vividly awake, and this alert quality naturally spills over into
activity in the form of focused energy and dynamism.

Along with that greater calm and alertness comes greater clarity.
Some people always seem to have confusion buzzing around them—
you walk into their house or office and it's as if someone has churned
the air with an eggbeater. The atmosphere feels so muddled that it's
hard to make a simple, direct statement without it splintering into
chaos on its way to your listeners' ears. Some people, on the other
hand, radiate so much clarity that when you're around them your own
thoughts are clearer, and things that seemed complicated resolve into
simplicity. You may have noticed that you're becoming a little more
like that second kind of person; if you haven't noticed it yet, stick
around.

As a result of this greater clarity, when one approach to a problem
doesn't work, you waste less time banging your head against the closed
door. You're quicker to notice that there's another door down the hall,
or maybe a window you can climb through. This clarity may first become evident in the workplace, where one garbled phone message or
ambiguously worded email can set off a ricochet effect that keeps zing-
ing around for hours or days, with time wasted, effort duplicated, re-
sentment brewed, and blame generously distributed. Sometimes just
an extra pinch of clarity at the outset is enough to prevent the whole

chaotic chain reaction. Carpenters say, "Measure twice, cut once." These days, you might not have time to measure twice, but with a little more clarity you can measure right the first time.

BREAKING OUT

At home, a similar thing may be happening with you and your partner. Your sharpened sensitivity might help you notice some annoying habit you've got, and how surprisingly easy it would be to drop it. Relationships are quick-turnaround feedback systems, aka instant karma: positive change usually sparks positive response, which in turn sparks more positive change.

That can help both of you break out of the vicious circles that couples often get caught in. Before, one partner might have done some dumb, inconsiderate thing—leaving dirty dishes in the sink or making insensitive jokes or criticizing his partner in front of other people. The partner gets angry and finds ways to dole out punishment, perhaps by withholding sex. (Smoldering anger makes people, understandably, not in the mood.) This negative feedback makes the first partner feel more alienated and hurt—I may as well leave *more* dishes in the sink, and round and round we go. There's no good outcome to this circle: they may get divorced, there may be some fooling around, or they may stick together for the kids and occasionally drop cutting, half-disguised comments at the dinner table that ensure that the kids are primed to continue the cycle into the next generation.

You don't have to be a genius to look around and see such patterns in other couples, yet few people stop to ask, "Hmmm, am *I* doing that?" They're so caught up that they don't notice that they're caught up. All of a sudden you're lashing out, and there doesn't seem to have been a moment when you could have opted not to. It's sad because you may truly love each other, and the whole soap opera is so unnecessary. But now our growing clarity and equanimity give us a better chance of sensing those moments when we can break the cycle of reactivity. Even as the soap opera unfolds, somehow the stage on which it unfolds becomes roomier, less claustrophobic, and we see the space where we can choose the other way. Certainly, breaking out is easiest if both partners are doing some kind of meditative practice, but even one can be enough. It takes two to tangle, and one to untangle.

Which brings us to a point of caution. In your enthusiasm for the greater peace and openness meditation is bringing to your life, it's tempting to pressure your partner to join in. *Don't do it.* It rarely works. It usually backfires. Also resist any temptation to evangelize your friends, colleagues, and near or distant relatives. In my early days I turned off a lot of people that way. Just be cool, and be cool with others not being cool. Keep doing your own practice, become the best possible example of what the stuff does, and, when they're ready, the others will ask *you* why you don't get upset or depressed or baffled when everyone else does. "By their fruits ye shall know them," says the Good Book.

Yes, it can be particularly tricky when one partner actively *resists* the other's practice, or even mocks it: "Sorry dinner's late, folks. Looks like Little Miss Buddha got stuck in her cave. Har har har." (Ladies, on behalf of all the lunkheaded guys of the world, I apologize.) Hang in there, *never* even hint that he should join you, and eventually, as it dawns on him how much smoother and more fun the relationship has become, he'll be guarding the door of your cave. In his own time, he might even join you.

You may notice your dealings with *everyone* improving. A common report is that our compulsion to push other people's buttons diminishes, and our own buttons seem to get smaller, harder for others to push. This can have big consequences. Gary, one of my students in prison, had served twenty-eight years and managed to reform himself quite beautifully. When I started working with him he had already had six unsuccessful appearances before the parole board. Each time, they managed to get a rise out of him. After a few years of meditation practice he had his seventh appearance, and, as he told me later, "They kept trying to find the buttons, but they weren't there anymore." He was released and is now a peaceful, productive member of society.

MIND AND BODY

Some of the changes may be physiological. People with medical conditions, especially stress-related conditions such as asthma or hypertension, often find them easing up. If you're on medication, you may feel that you can reduce your dosage, but of course you should check with your doctor first. You may find that you're sleeping better. You may also find that you're dreaming more. That's usually a result of emotional or neurological discharge that's stirred up in meditation and is most common early on. It's a good thing.

Back pain often has a strong psychogenic factor, which doesn't mean that it's all in the mind but that it *starts* in the mind. So now it may begin to ease up—if we lean into the turn, as on the Vespa. Some clinical researchers, notably Dr. John Sarno, have observed that most back pain arises as a reaction to suppressed emotions such as fear or rage.

Rather than acknowledge these feelings, we unconsciously tighten the back to distract ourselves from them, depriving the area of oxygen-rich blood so that the muscles go into spasm.

So if you have back problems, you can try taking advantage of the freer, less conditioned awareness that meditation has opened up. When your back starts to twinge, don't focus on the pain; instead, immediately ask yourself what emotion is trying to get your attention. Then just notice the answer that arises, allowing the emotion to be there without resistance or judgment. As you find out that it's OK to have those feelings, the old distraction mechanism loses its rationale and the pain falls away. It may sound far-fetched, but I've personally known several people who have found great relief this way. One friend had crippling back pain for six years, tried many kinds of conventional and alternative treatments without success, finally applied this method for a week and a half, and became permanently pain-free.

ALL ABOUT Z

There's always 360 degrees of stuff going on around us, the report of the five senses as well as our thoughts and feelings. But of this 360 degrees we usually pick out some segment of, let's say, 10 degrees, some object or idea—let's call it z—and decide that it matters more than the other 350. We invest z with more energy than the rest, more charge, whether positive or negative, and fix our attention on it. This is called *fixation*, and it happens most of the time, whether we fixate on something we think we need or on something we think we need to get rid of. When it becomes extreme or even pathological, it's called obsession.

In a sense, meditation is an exercise in nonfixation. The dog barks, the bus rolls by, thoughts come and go, feelings come and go, and we don't engage with any of it. As long as we're in our meditation seat, we've decided that it doesn't matter what we experience, what we think, what we feel. Sometimes, by force of habit, we do engage for a while, and think, "Jeez, if only that ceiling fan would stop squeaking, then I'd be fine," or, "If only I were done with this meditation and watching the Cubs game, I'd be happy." But then we remember the instruction and let go again into the space of neutrality, of being OK with whatever.

To discover a space of neutrality like that, a haven of OK-ness, of nothing lacking and nothing mattering—even for a few minutes—is a huge deal. It begins to undermine the whole mechanism of fixation. The more thoroughly we marinate in that space of freedom, the less we'll fixate on things during the rest of the day. So the neighbor's dog barks for a few minutes, or you've got a hangnail that needs trimming, or you wish that cute girl at work would smile at you, or the kid upstairs with the new guitar won't stop playing "Hotel California." Fine. You develop a more relaxed sense of humor about it all, and a mellower, more mature, 360-degree, big-picture perspective.

You can still focus sharply when necessary, but focus is a choice, an assertion of freedom. Fixation is slavery, whether you're engrossed in the latest political horror show that's beyond your control or you're losing sleep over your old boyfriend's crummy behavior, which he has long since forgotten. There comes a point when we're just tired of those chains, and now they're loosening up.

IT'S ME

There's a Zen fable on this point. A monk finds himself fixating on a spider that dangles in front of his face every time he meditates. He finally goes to the *roshi*, the Zen master, and asks to borrow his knife to kill the spider. "Sure thing," says the roshi, "but first take this piece of chalk and mark an *X* on the spider's belly." The monk complies, then returns to ask again for the knife. "Sure thing," says the roshi, "but first lift up your robe." There, on the monk's belly, is a big chalk *X*. "Good thing I didn't give you that knife," says the roshi.

It's not the spider (or the Cubs game, or the boyfriend). It's us. If you understand that, you understand the Buddha's Four Noble Truths.

1. We've been suffering.

2. Our suffering doesn't come from outside. We generate it by fixating.

3. Therefore, we can stop suffering by letting go of fixation.

4. We can cultivate the habit of letting go by living a meditative life.

In case you're interested, that's the entire Buddhist philosophy in a nutshell. It all comes down to saying to the universe, "It's not you, it's me"... and then dropping the fixation that was *making* it you. We'll still have pain, but that's different. Even lawsuits differentiate between pain and suffering. Pain, as the saying goes, is mandatory; suffering is optional. As long as we're in physical bodies, we're subject to pain, but it's up to us whether to add the extra sauce of suffering. When your car breaks down on your way to a movie, you can choose to suffer by fixating on the movie you're missing and the mechanic's bill you'll have to pay, digging deeper and deeper into your story of woe. Or you can enjoy the stars and the crickets while you wait for the tow truck. Either way, you'll be spending the same amount of time on the shoulder.

Researchers at Walter Reed National Military Medical Center have found that they can successfully treat the "phantom pain" some veterans have in amputated limbs by placing a mirror alongside the remaining limb. The patient practices unclenching the muscles in the mirrored limb, and the pain diminishes. I think the Buddha would take this as a metaphor for our own situation. We suffer (First Noble Truth) because we're all clenching phantom limbs, tightening ourselves around phantom situations (Second Noble Truth) that are in the vanished past or the imagined future or simply out of our control. We stop suffering when we learn to unclench (Third Noble Truth), which we do by meditating and continuing to lean into the openness of meditative space (Fourth Noble Truth).

If you think this sounds a bit like the Serenity Prayer of Twelve-Step fame—"God, grant me the serenity to accept the things I cannot change, the courage to change the things I can, and wisdom to know the difference"—you're right. Millions of people have heard that prayer, prayed it earnestly, and perhaps found their burdens eased. But many still find themselves unserenely banging their heads against the things they can't change. Through meditation, we grant *ourselves* the necessary serenity, courage, and wisdom—or, if you prefer, we place ourselves in a position to humbly accept God's grant.

THE ROOT OF ADDICTION

Speaking of Twelve Steps: If you don't have any addictive behaviors, congratulations. If you do, have you noticed that their grip has loosened up a bit? We can be talking about anything from full-blown, heavy-duty substance abuse to the compulsive need to leave the TV playing all day or to check your messages every five minutes. Just as with any addiction, we keep acting as if the *next* message or tweet (or cigarette or bonbon or shot or drink or poker hand or reckless sexual encounter) will be the one that's so fabulous we'll die of pleasure and never need another. Rationally, we know it's not true, but we take the hook anyway. That's why it's called addiction.

Evidence has been accumulating for decades that meditation can reduce addiction, and researchers explain it in terms of measurable phenomena like increased blood flow to the anterior cingulate cortex, a part of the brain involved with self-control. Fine. As usual, though, I prefer the inner, subjective, experiential perspective. If you could grab the next hundred people you meet, sit them down, inject them with truth serum, and have them pour out their deepest feelings about life, many of them would describe it as essentially grim: flat, bleak, dry, life's a bitch and then you die, empty to empty, zero to zero, game over. That grimness remains the default status of life till we fill it with stimuli or dull it with depressants, and whenever we let up we have to face the grimness again. So if we find a reliable delivery mechanism, it makes perfect sense that we'll keep pushing the lever.

Trying to address addiction when we feel in our bones that life is grim is like trying to jog to California up the aisle of a bus that's barreling toward New York. But there's something that can upend that worldview, and its seed is contained in a deceptively simple experience you may have already had. You're meditating, not much seems to be happening, but then perhaps your cat jumps on you or your phone rings or your alarm tells you it's time to go to work . . . *and you don't want to come out.* You're just sitting, just being, but now you realize there's something delicious about just being—so delicious that, in this moment, nothing can entice you to come out voluntarily.

When you finally get your eyes open, the memory of that moment may fade, but still something life changing has happened. You've experienced the essential deliciousness of beingness itself. There's no opiate, no stimulus—no high score on Guitar Hero, no steak or martini, no Twinkies or Ding Dongs, no orgasm or Cirque du Soleil—but you just want to keep marinating in it. Perhaps the most memorable thing I ever heard my old teacher Maharishi say was in Fiuggi, Italy, in 1972. I was in a group of a few hundred students, at the end of a retreat of several months, meeting with him in the *teatro* in the center of town. Sitting on the stage in his teaching seat, dressed as always in his white monk's robe, he chuckled softly into his beard as he searched for words to express this most remarkable, completely inexpressible fact of life. Finally he said:

"It's just . . . *nothing.* But there's something very good about it."

This something very good, this non-grim, no-artificial-flavors-needed inherent nature of life, is called *ananda*—bliss—in Hindu philosophy. Buddhists call it *eka-rasa*, the One Taste running through all experience. I like the word I've learned from my Dutch relatives: *lekker*, meaning yummy, delicious (like the English word *delectable*). In Holland, they don't limit its use to food, because, like the Hindus and Buddhists, they understand that it's a quality that can be found anywhere. When they tuck their kids into bed, they say, "*Slaap lekker*," sleep yummy. (And when they *really* like something, it's *lekker gezellig*, "yummy cozy.")

That one I-don't-wanna-come-out moment of meditation, even if it's later half-forgotten, means you've tasted the same ananda as all the enlightened sages. Sure, you've just nibbled it and they've fully digested it, but you're on your way, irreversibly. You've started to notice that existence itself is not grim but lekker, and to that extent the root of your addiction has been pulled up. Certainly, keep using whatever else helps you stay clean and sober, as long as you still need it, whether it's your AA meetings or Antisocial—an app that temporarily blocks your access to Facebook or any other site you designate as a rabbit hole.

IT'S NICE TO BE NICE

Another addiction, not usually recognized as such, is that of carping, complaining, whining, *kvetching* (to use the Sanskrit term). You rarely have to look far to see people aggravating their own aggravations, like someone compulsively scratching a mosquito bite. The other day I was on an upper floor of an office building, waiting for the elevator. Three older ladies were waiting with me. They shifted about uncomfortably, looking for something to rest their gaze on in the empty corridor. One of them whined, "Why do these things take so *long*?" We had been there for under a minute, but I could see that they had already grumbled it into an hour. For me, the corridor also contained nothing . . . but, as Maharishi would say, there was something very good about it. My friend David sells commercial real estate in the Midwest. Once I overheard him on his cell phone, working a deal. "Yeah, it's in the middle of nowhere," he said, "but it's a *beautiful* middle of nowhere." That's it.

It's all Second Noble Truth, propagation of needless suffering, and of course it's always easier to see in others than in ourselves. But as we start recognizing the muscle memory of that perverse exercise, we can start letting it go and making room for its opposite. When you pull up to the red light that you wanted to be green, you might notice that you're projecting your stress onto that stupid traffic light and the whole stupid intersection. You might notice that you're squeezing the steering wheel, trying to make the light turn green *now*. But you may also notice that none of this helps. The traffic light, strangely ignoring your displeasure, turns green exactly when it's good and ready, and you drive off to the next red light—the next opportunity to catch the pattern a little earlier and relax into the clearing a little sooner.

As this clearing opens up, it improves life for others as well. We've been projecting stress not only onto objects like traffic lights but also onto people. We may have been getting off on making other people not just wrong but goddamn stupid idiots, and that's a toxic drug that does to your heart what meth does to your face. On a global scale, tribes and nations with twisted hearts prepare to pounce, projecting the worst possible motives onto each other, because look—*they're* preparing to pounce.

We can't change all of this, but we can change our little corner, and that's a start. We've all, for example, griped about getting stuck on the phone with the customer service rep from hell. When you're graced with a rep who's clear and pleasant, you can thank her for that and tell her what a difference she's made for you. You'll hear her brighten up, and you'll know you've made her day. How many other ways can you do that kind of thing? Try seeing how many people's day you can make, and then see how that makes you feel. If enough of us did that, the world might be different.

People ridiculed the 1930s spiritual leader Father Divine when he reported that his great revelation from God was, "It's nice to be nice." But that's a profound message. When you're nice to other people, it feels nice in your own nervous system. Niceness is lekker: it has some of the same delicious flavor as ananda, bliss. Gradually, we recognize that the blissful eyes-closed glow of meditation and the blissful eyes-open glow of kind, generous, nice behavior are the same glow. If you're good, you go to heaven; that is, when you act nice, you feel nice. If you go to heaven, naturally you're good; that is, when you feel nice from soaking in ananda, you spontaneously act nice.

TRUE CONCENTRATION

With some meditation under your belt, it also becomes easier to concentrate on things like work and school. Spontaneous, natural concentration turns out to feel very different from the tense mental rigidity most people associate with that word. Your I-don't-wanna-come-out-of-meditation moment happened because the blissful ananda had enticed you into concentration, which is not a task but a state. Now you're starting to pick up on that flavor elsewhere, everywhere. Even algebra homework has some taste of lekker. Even quarterly reports have some taste of lekker. As the legendary football coach George "Papa Bear" Halas said, "Nothing is work unless you'd rather be doing something else." Because natural meditation means just relaxing into what's always already there, we find that that delicious quality is still available after we leave the cushion, no matter what we're doing. Meditation is like what geologists do when they drill a core sample of the earth, going deep in one spot to find a layer that underlies all spots.

In traditional societies, people were fascinated by superbeings with superpowers. (They still are, as a matter of fact.) Also, most people couldn't read, so wisdom teachings about the potentialities of human existence were encoded in the stories and images of the heroes and gods. Lord Ganesha, who is so popular in India that I've seen his picture pop up on ATMs to offer his blessing along with my cash, has several instructive attributes. One is his massive elephant's head, which represents the vastness of enlightened awareness. Another is a bowl of sweets he holds in his left hand (*one* of his left hands, that is), like the *gulab jamun* you may have had for dessert in Indian restaurants: balls of fried milk curd swimming in an intensely sweet syrup.

Ganesha's sweets represent the delectable ananda quality of exis-

Ganesha's Mouse

tence. On the ground, right under the bowl, is a mouse, representing the thinking mind. Like a hungry mouse, our mind usually scurries to and fro, looking for crumbs and scraps to satisfy it. But Ganesha's mouse is at rest, enjoying the sweet syrup that drips from the bowl. This is precisely how the mind comes into the state of natural, spontaneous concentration, first during our sitting sessions and eventually anywhere we want it to. No mousetraps are required. No mice were harmed in the making of this joyous life.

Quietly, inconspicuously, you start being happy for no particular reason. Sure, in the outer world you still have preferences—given a choice between spending the next few hours waiting for an elevator or watching *City Lights*, I'll take the movie, thank you very much—but there's a growing awareness that that bowl of dripping sweets is right above you wherever you are, so wherever you are is fine. Possibly the best compliment I ever received was from the late Jack Dufford, a colleague of mine when I taught English. One day at lunch he said, "You know, Dean, everybody has a happy place, but your happy place is wherever you are." That's what happens. Increasingly, everyplace is happy place and every hour is happy hour. It's a pleasure to be here.

This transformation is a cumulative process. That's a good thing, because life is unpredictable. Having that delicious taste when you're waiting for an elevator is useful; it will be indispensable when the tsunami hits, or when the grid goes down and our infotainment systems and sewage systems stop working. And whether or not that happens on a mass scale in your lifetime, a time will come when your own personal grid goes down, when your body's infotainment and sewage systems stop working. Meditation is insurance against the day when you'd *better* be happy just being, because you can't do much else.

DECISIONS AND OMISSIONS

You may also notice that decision-making is getting easier. Specifically, it becomes less mental—less *thinking* and more *knowing*. When I was twelve, I took up chess for a while, but each time my opponent pushed a pawn I tried to mentally work through every possible response I could make, his every possible response to my every possible response, my every possible response to his every possible response to my every possible response, and so on. All those possible responses quickly branched out into . . . well, into pounding head pressure. Eventually, I learned to look at the board, see more, and think less—to sit back, see the overall patterns, and somehow *feel* where the strengths and weaknesses and openings were. The feedback that told me my new approach was right was that the head pressure went away and I won more games.

Meditation does that to your chess game of life. We start to see where the openings are, and we flow through them. At first, we may be so used to going round and round the mulberry bush of thoughts that it's a shock to just see and know rather than think and think. But as we shift more into this new way of functioning and find that it works, we come to trust it. We stop trying to figure out life and *live* life.

Sometimes this path of intuitive right decision-making is more a matter of omission than commission. Socrates said he was guided by an inner voice that never told him what to do but warned him what not to do. It advised him, for example, not to go into politics—a single no that probably enhanced his total happiness quotient more than any several hundred yeses. The comedian Sam Levenson once said, "It's so simple to be wise. . . . Just think of something stupid to say, and then don't say it."

In one moment we can do or say one dumb thing with explosive consequences, then spend years mopping up the mess. The problem is, we're slow on the uptake, and we've done or said that dumb thing before we know it. Now perhaps our neurons fire a little faster, and we have the extra half-second grace period in which to not do or say it.

INDEPENDENT OBSERVERS

Some of the results of meditation have a way of sneaking up on you. One evening you realize that you've stopped automatically pouring that second glass of wine at dinner. You don't know when it happened, but you no longer need it to feel relaxed at the end of the day.

Sometimes others see the changes more clearly from the outside than we can from the inside. Often people tell new meditators that they have a sort of fresh, just-washed-your-face look. And sometimes it's more extreme than that. Once, years ago in Philadelphia, I was leading a refresher session for people who had started meditation a few months earlier. A very large middle-aged woman in a floral-print dress plunked herself down in the middle of the front row. Beside her was her husband, a balding, meek-looking little guy. Together they looked like a barge and a tugboat.

Pretty soon she started raising her hand, objecting to everything I was saying, and complaining in her foghorn voice, "This stupid stuff doesn't work. I've been doing it religiously for three months now, and nothing's happened. You should be ashamed of yourself, scamming people like this." Afraid she was going to demoralize the others, I tried to placate her, but she wasn't buying. I limped through the session as best I could. At the end, as people were starting to leave, the husband managed to break free and sidled up to me. "There's something you should know," he whispered. "*She's crazy.*" He looked over his shoulder; she was still putting on her coat. "*But . . .* for the first time in thirty years, I can stand to live with her!"

Hmmm. Was the change in the wife, the husband, or both? My money is on both, but who knows? The Buddha always refused to take on speculative questions, patiently repeating, "I'm just here to address suffering and the elimination of suffering." In those terms, I think I had a pretty good day.

ZOOM ZOOM

To whatever degree you've noticed these first glimmers, this sun is just rising. There's much more to come. But even a faint glimmer can make a big difference. The Bhagavad Gita says, "Even a little of this process delivers one from great fear." Once you know the direction you're headed, just keep your foot on the pedal and your eventual arrival is assured. And there are some nice, supercharged engine additives waiting for you in the coming chapters.

Whether or not you can say for sure that you've noticed greater calm, or clarity, or freedom from addiction, or anything else, the most significant glimmer may be a faint sense of *something* that doesn't change, an inkling of something indefinable that's not affected by the ups and downs of daily life. It's not just a passing mood or thought, but the simple, underlying awareness that's more open and spacious and *free* than any mood or thought. You may find yourself wondering, "Is this really happening or am I just psyching myself out?" That's fine. Hang on to your skepticism as long as you can. Once again, be a good scientist—but that means conduct well-designed experiments. You've already done the control test: all those years of life without meditation. Now give meditation enough time to show what it can do. Even if just to prove me wrong, you'll have to sit regularly.

11. Meditating on Vacancy

I had a visit the other day from an old friend, whom I'll call Edwin. He's a great guy, but his personality can be, let's say, a tad on the incendiary side. After a round of coffee and a pleasant chat, it was time for him to go. I started walking him out across my deck toward the back gate, where he had parked his bike. I was about to point out a new little garden Buddha that my wife had just added to the yard, nestled among the shrubbery, but Edwin had launched into a long rant about rude, inconsiderate shoppers who block the aisles of the local Whole Foods, failing to see him coming with his cart as they self-indulgently study organic olive oil labels. At some point this morphed into a tirade against rude, inconsiderate motorists who endanger his safety by failing to give his bike the legally mandated three-foot clearance. When I could finally get a word in, I gently suggested that, as the word *inconsiderate* implies, they probably didn't consider what they were doing and how it affected others. Perhaps they weren't bad people, simply oblivious—they just didn't see him.

Edwin was having none of it. Their behavior was a moral failing, it revealed their flawed character, they were the schmucks who were responsible for the decline of Western civilization. *He*, on the other hand, always made it a point to be considerate and aware, to treat his environment as he expected to be treated. . . . At this point he suddenly stopped in midsentence, turned away from me, and spat into the trees.

"'Scuse me," he said. "Couple of coffee grounds."

"Uh, Edwin?" I said. "This is our new Buddha . . . that you just spat on."

A look of utter mortification came over him—and then we both started laughing. It was too perfect. Neither of us had to mention the rich irony of his having demonstrated exactly the heedlessness that he was ready to hang everyone else for. Still laughing, we just looked wildly into each other's eyes. To Edwin's great credit—to his great *delight*—rather than doubling down, casting about for ever more creaky, implausible logic to prop up his heroic-me-against-the-barbaric-world narrative, he watched it all come crashing down and relished the big boom. And for at least that moment, he savored the empty space that was left in its place, the fresh breeze that blew through it, the relief when there was suddenly no more story to sustain.

Edwin had stumbled into a rare blessing: a chance to see, before doing too much damage, that he was full of shit. And also that he was the Buddha, and that all the schmucks who spat on him in various ways were, like him, just well-meaning, blundering mortals. Of course we're all mortals, *and* Buddhas, *and* full of shit, and can perhaps share in Edwin's blessing by drawing some perspective from his story.

The real blessing here is the sudden revelation of the now-vacated space where our narrative used to be. Whether it's a political position, a religious conviction, a dietary theory, a family drama, or a relationship soap opera, we love for us to be right and for the others to be wrong. We'll usually work overtime to prop up our feeling of rightness, even when we have to engage in protracted kitchen battles or Facebook wars . . . and even when a sneaking suspicion in some corner of our mind starts to whisper that, ya know, this time we might be wrong. *Especially* then.

So here's a suggestion:

The next time your story starts to blow up, let it blow. You've already tried defending your stories to the death, possibly for most of your life. This time, just once, try gratefully offering it up and see what happens. You'll probably live. And you'll probably notice an exhilarating spaciousness where the story used to be. We've all experienced, when we're *literally* full of shit and then get thoroughly, satisfyingly emptied out, that suddenly our step is lighter and the world is a sunnier place. It's something like that for consciousness.

There are other kinds of narratives as well, that don't depend on the right/wrong dynamic. I just got a call from another old friend, updating me at great, great length on her harrowing medical history, blow by blow by blow. "No, wait a minute. *Then* they took me off the codeine, and *then* they stuck me for a new central line." At the same time, it was clear how much energy she had invested in *curating* her narrative, keeping all the details in order, living and reliving even the ones that were past.

Yes, I know, that's the way most people deal with illness. But there's another way, and I was schooled in it by Maggy, my first wife. When she developed cancer, we got the best medical advice available, dealt with each new development as intelligently as we knew how, and then dropped it as much as we could. At Maggy's insistence, we avoided telling anyone outside the immediate family for as long as possible, after she discovered how tedious it was going over and over the story with people—"carrying everybody else's emotional baggage," as she put it—and hearing all their well-meaning stories about every aunt of theirs who'd ever had a tumor. That way, for the months of life she had left, not every moment had to be about cancer. Emptied of that story, some of it could just be about life.

What does all this have to do with meditation?

Any encounter with exhilarating, luminous emptiness—Buddhists call it *shunyata*—goes to the core of what meditation is about. As meditators, we don't have to wait for the next time we get sick or spit in the wrong place to have such an encounter. The procedure is simple. . . .

~

Sit in your preferred position. Stretch and settle in as usual.

Now recall a situation where you worked too hard at maintaining some narrative. Maybe back in high school or college you got heavily invested in an image of yourself as Suffering Poet or Joe Studly. Or maybe this week you've been sitting up nights, worrying about some issue at work you're afraid you'll get blamed for or come into conflict over.

Whatever it is, summon it up. Think about it, dwell on it, let yourself get completely wrapped up in it—and then suddenly blow it up. This doesn't mean to try to systematically deconstruct it with the mind. In this endeavor, the mind is not your friend; it's the one that's been doing the mischief. Just see the whole constructed edifice of the story as a big *thing*, like a massive skyscraper, and, as in the climax of some slam-bam Hollywood action film, blow the sucker up. Kablooey!

And then abide in the cool, free vacant space that remains. *Rest* in that space. Ahhhhhhh!

That space is now your object of meditation, and by now you know how to rest in any object of meditation: just letting go and letting be, not trying to change or manipulate the experience, allowing thoughts and sounds to come and go in the background. In this case, thoughts related to the old narrative may bubble up. Doubts may bubble up: "Wait a minute—was I right or wrong on this one?" For now, it doesn't matter. Treat those thoughts like any others, neither suppressing nor engaging them, just disregarding them. We've all seen that Hollywood shot where, as the building blows up behind him, the hero just keeps walking toward the camera, cool as hell. Don't even turn around.

At some point, if you feel really ready to go hard-core, try this:

Sit down, settle in, and then assume, just for the duration of this session, that *all* your rationales, *all* your interpretations, *all* your carefully maintained narratives have turned out to be bullshit. Blow it *all* up. Ahhhhhhhhhhhhhhhhhhhhhhhhhhhhhh!

That leaves a big, *big* space to rest in. Enjoy, my friend!

Of course, you have your Double-O license to blow it all up because you know that you've merely checked your stories at the door, and can always pick them up again on the way out. But maybe this feels so good that you won't want to. A friend of mine who's dieting has a Post-it on her refrigerator door on which she's written, "Nothing tastes as good as thin feels." You may discover that none of your drivel tastes as good as vacancy feels.

~

This kind of practice starts to familiarize us with liberative emptiness, shunyata, which, it is said, underlies and pervades all of existence. Being good scientists, we'll have to check in the research lab of our own lives whether that's the case. There are many ways to approach that emptiness, eighty-four thousand according to Buddhist tradition, although that may just be a poetically large number. But whichever way you get there, it's the same destination. (And it's the same as what, in other traditions, is called by the other names we've used. It's the *only* destination.)

Also, as you develop a taste for space rather than narrative—as you see that it tastes great *and* is less filling—you become less inclined to invest in *new* narratives. You've tried out this more spacious mode of being, but only within the safe behind-the-closed-eyelids environment of meditation. Now you may start finding yourself emboldened to drop your creaky old narratives in real life, whatever they may be: Mom was a narcissist, Dad liked my brother better, I was always the last kid picked for kickball, I always screw things up. And—perhaps with a little chuckle—you'll decline to pick up new narratives as they spray on their cheap perfume and seductively call your name. No thank you, my dear . . . maybe some other time . . . but probably not.

Part of this process is noticing that the feeling of being *right* is indeed a feeling, a sensation, that may have nothing to do with the reality of the world outside your skin. But the longer an idea stays lodged in your head, the more that sensation of rightness is reinforced, like money earning interest, till you're *positive*—a more intense and addictive version of the feeling. Whenever such a long-held conviction is challenged (perhaps pointed out by your partner as she helpfully busts your chops), it's like yanking the pacifier out of a baby's mouth. You may become defensive, even angry.

This is a precious opportunity. You can save yourself from getting completely caught up in reactivity by noting that those feelings of anger and defensiveness are *also* merely sensations. They're not you—*you* are not threatened. Notice what they feel like in the body. Don't suppress them, don't buy into them, just watch them with loving, detached interest, and soon you'll feel the vacancy open up beneath them. As you realize how unlikely it is that you're the first person in the history of the universe to be right 100 percent of the time—that that's not in your job description—you'll breathe a lot easier.

12. States

To be conscious is a miracle. To have *human* consciousness is a stunning, staggering miracle; the odds against it are astronomical. It's said that the Buddha once pushed his thumb into the ground, brought up a little mound of dirt on his thumbnail, and held it aloft for his monks to see. "If all the dirt in the world represents all the forms in which we could be born," he said, "the bit of dirt on my thumbnail represents your chances of being born as a human." Kurt Vonnegut struck a similar note in *Cat's Cradle*, where he invented the Caribbean-island religion of Bokononism. One passage of its scripture reads:

> God made mud.
> God got lonesome.
> So God said to some of the mud, "Sit up!"
> "See all I've made," said God, "the hills, the sea, the sky, the stars."
> And I was some of the mud that got to sit up and look around.
> Lucky me, lucky mud.

Just to have ordinary, garden-variety human consciousness is unspeakably extraordinary. We are the luckiest of mud. No need to consider further: we'd be perfectly justified to stop right here with tears of wonder and gratitude pouring down our cheeks.

But let's consider further.

⁓

In the course of a day, ordinary human consciousness takes the form of three states: waking, dreaming, and (dreamless) sleep. Each has a distinct, objectively measurable set of symptoms, such as oxygen consumption, eye movement, and brain wave function. They're also distinct subjectively—three fundamentally different modes of experiencing.

As we've noted before, the waking state is alert and active. That is, consciousness is both switched on, so to speak, so that it's *capable* of entertaining various experiences, and constantly engaged, *having* those experiences. It encounters the sights, sounds, smells, tastes, and textures of what we call the outer world—all the stuff that lucky mud gets to meet. It also generates thoughts and feelings about those experiences and shuttles from one to another, seeking fulfillment from them. It's as if we switch on the TV, so that the screen glows, watch as that glow takes the form of shows about our daytime world—news reports, nature programs, "reality" shows—and keep up a running commentary on what we see. And we keep clicking the remote, hoping to find something good on.

In the dream state, consciousness is neither at rest nor truly alert. The five senses continue to function, but now they project alternate worlds, within which the mind continues to bounce from one experience to the next. Here the experiences are, well, dreamy—hazier, and often funnier or scarier than in the waking state, and usually forgotten immediately. Dreaming is sort of like switching on the TV, seeing the screen glow dimly and intermittently, and with some difficulty watching a mash-up of fake news, cartoons, and vampire dramas. Still we channel-surf, ever seeking fulfillment, sometimes finding exotic pleasures unavailable in the waking state, sometimes encountering more intense frustrations and terrors.

In the dreamless sleep state, as it's ordinarily experienced, consciousness is at rest but not alert. There's nothing on TV. On paper, it might sound like the least desirable, most boring, most deathlike state. And yet we're all attracted to it—everyone loves a good, deep sleep. We might argue that we love it only indirectly, for its refreshing effect on the waking state the next morning, but it's more than that. Sleep is the one state in which we don't seek fulfillment. Free of past and future and even present, free from nagging hopes and fears, free from the endless effort to figure life out, we're in a state of perfect peace, perfect inner quietude. The tormented insomniac Macbeth calls it "innocent sleep," as it is pure, virginal, unsullied by our conflicts, ambitions, and opinions. When you're in deep sleep, are you a liberal or a conservative? What's your religion? How much personal history do you drag behind you? You're free of all that weight. But you're also unconscious, so you don't actually *experience* that innocent peace. Even so, we're irresistibly drawn to its healing power: Macbeth also calls it the "balm of hurt minds."

What the ancient yogis discovered in their meditation is a fourth state. They called it, among other things, *turiya* (toor-EE-ya), which literally means "the fourth." Almost mathematically inevitable, it's the one remaining possibility, where consciousness is fully at rest, passive, yet fully alert. Nothing's on, but the screen glows bright. This state offers the perfect repose, the nothing-lacking, no-unfulfillment, no-past-present-future of the dreamless sleep state, but we're conscious—we're awake and alert to *enjoy* it.

If you've been meditating for some days now, you've at least dipped your toe into this fourth state, and perhaps gone right in over your head. It may have been only for brief moments, and at this stage the experience may be pretty vague. It's common for new meditators to think they were just sleeping, because, till now, sleep is the only state they've known in which the mind rests. But if you cross-examine them, you may find out that their head didn't fall forward, they continued to be dimly aware of sounds in the background, and so forth. Frequently the report goes something like, "Some time passed, but I had no idea how much, and I wasn't sure what had happened, but afterward I felt invigorated." Or, "I don't know where I was, but when I came out I felt good, and somehow everything seemed . . . fresh, washed, like the streets and trees after the rain." Or, "When I opened my eyes, I was surprised to find myself sitting in a room, or even being in a body." When I guide a meditation and we discuss it afterward, I'm always happy when someone says, "Oh, were you talking? Well, I guess you were there somewhere in the background, but I didn't really hear you. Anyway, anything you could say would have been superfluous."

Turiya is the just-nothing-but-something-very-good-about-it state Maharishi spoke of, where we're marinating in the essential deliciousness of existence. It's the *real* balm of hurt minds. Again, because the experience is new, it can seem more like a blank at first, as if our eyes have to get used to the light. It can seem like a dropout of missing time, because, as a matter of fact, it's a dropping into timelessness. Actually, it's not strictly correct to call it a state, as states are passing things that change through time: rather, it's a window into the changeless being-ness that underlies all the changing states—the I-awareness we ex-plored in Chapter 1. In sleep, we're unaware; in dreaming and waking, we're aware of experiences; in turiya, we're resting as awareness itself, the experienc*er*. It's a glimpse of the core of our existence, which is al-ways there, always us, whether we glimpse it or not.

As we continue to alternate meditation and activity, these glimpses begin to carry over. If you dunk a dry sponge into a bucket of water, it comes out wet. And with *this* sponge, if you keep on dunking it, one day it stops drying out. Our glimpses of the silent, changeless substrate of awareness, both in and out of meditation, start connecting up. It dawns on us, with growing clarity, that turiya has always been the background of every moment. Increasingly—whether we're vacationing in Bali or commuting from Hackensack, whether we're lapping up sweet dreams or tossing in feverish nightmares—all the complicated drama of our life's comedy and tragedy is seen to take place upon the stage of per-fect, delicious, simple peace, boundless awareness-space. Does this re-alization turn us into the clichéd passive meditator, withdrawing from the activity of the world with a blissful, silly grin? Nope. In fact, the more unshakably we're established in the silence, the more vigorously and skillfully we can plunge into the drama. Go, dogs, go!

With this understanding of the three states of consciousness and the fourth, stateless state, a clearer view of the end point of our meditation starts coming into focus. We've all heard and possibly used words like *nirvana* and *enlightenment*, but perhaps with only a vague sense of what they might mean, or an assumption that they refer to something very personal and subjective—my nirvana might feature large quantities of fresh whipped cream and dark chocolate, yours might come with hot sauce. But now we can even lay it out as a mathematical equation, as precise as Einstein's $E = mc^2$ . . . and just as disruptive of our old picture of existence.

$$E = T^p + (w, d, s)$$

That is, enlightenment equals turiya to the permanent power—pure awareness, objectless being, the true I, recognized perpetually—along with the ongoing rotation of waking, dreaming, and sleeping. The unbroken ahhhhhhh is never again lost to view, even in deep sleep. Those occasional moments in meditation that are so deeply, deliciously silent, such balm to our hurt minds that we don't want to come out, are portents of the day when we won't *have* to come out . . . even when we come out. More precisely, we'll see that we've never been out. We wake up and realize that we've always been safe at home in Kansas, dreaming we were lost in Oz.

Clarifying our understanding in this way can help us see the profound significance of the path we're walking, and keep us from being diverted onto side roads. Perhaps you started meditation just to relax a bit. Fine—it'll do that for you. But once you have even a kind of, sort of, almost, maybe quasi-clear vision of this destination, you'll keep going till you reach it.

13. Meditating into Sleep

Up till now we've focused on integrating meditation into the hours of the day when we're awake. That omits about a third of each twenty-four-hour cycle.

The yogis and lamas who, hundreds of years ago, dedicated their lives to attaining higher awareness through meditative practice weren't going to leave that big chunk of prime real estate undeveloped. They devised methods for opening to turiya during the sleep and dream states in addition to the waking state. Some of these approaches, such as the more advanced techniques of "dream yoga" expounded by certain schools of Tibetan Buddhism, are best practiced under the supervision of a teacher who specializes in them. But there are also basic nighttime techniques that you can do on your own, even as a newbie. This one is my favorite because it's the simplest, yet very powerful.

~

Start by turning off your lights as usual and then either sitting up in bed with a pillow or two behind you or else lying down, preferably on your back.

Close your eyes and let things settle naturally for a few moments.

Now notice the space inside you—your internal visual field.

You'll probably notice that this inner space is not completely dark: there's some faint sense of light glowing there.

Notice whether it has some vague color.

Notice whether the light is static or seems to be subtly shimmering or scintillating.

Continue to rest your attention in this way, in whatever vague sense of glowing space may be there. Don't try to sharpen your focus or see anything clearly. Just let it be as it is; rest in it as it is.

At first, it may seem as if this glowing space is confined by the shape and size of your head or body; after a while that boundedness tends to melt away, leaving only a pervasive glow with no perimeter. But however the experience changes or remains the same, let it change or remain the same.

As always, don't mind thoughts or anything else that presents itself. Let it go and let it be. Just rest easily in this subtle glow.

As you begin dissolving into sleep, you may find snippets of cartoony dream elements starting to appear, like little snatches of visual gibberish. As they take over, or as sleep takes over, your sense of the glow may start to slip away. Without straining, stay with it as long as possible; see if you can bring it into the sleep with you. It may seem as if you have to choose to go with either the glow or the sleep, but subtly feel out how to ride the glow *into* the sleep.

If you've been sitting up, when you realize you're falling asleep you'll probably want to slip down into the bed, while continuing to rest in the glow.

If you wake up during the night, just start this meditation again. If you have a history of broken sleep and are in the habit of reading to get drowsy, try doing this night meditation instead. Or if you wind up reading after all, do the meditation when you start to drop off and put your book aside.

∼

What's going on here?

As with all our explorations, the experience itself is ultimately its own explanation. But this technique of night meditation brings us into a new experiential dimension, and some explanation is in order.

Falling asleep, as we've done it in the past, is sort of like descending into a dark cave. In the ordinary experience of dreamless sleep, nothing's there, not even *awareness* that nothing's there—we're so utterly in the dark that we don't know we're in the dark. It's actually a pretty bizarre way to spend a third of your life.

Falling asleep while holding on to the glow is like going into the cave with a lamp. As we descend into the nothing, we retain some degree of consciousness. We start seeing in the dark—and, delightfully, there's nothing to see in the dark of the sleep state except our own light, the light of I-awareness. The deathlike inertness of sleep becomes the blissful peace of turiya.

When you first start to practice this night meditation, puzzling things may happen. You may have mornings when you think you haven't slept, but you feel deeply rested so you must have been asleep after all. *And awake*—but not awake in the insomniac's sense of turn-over-again, stare-at-the-ceiling, hear-the-clock-ticking awakeness. It's a different kind of awakeness that's timeless and not aware of any*thing*, yet still luminously aware. That's turiya.

You may also feel that you're dreaming less or more. Dreams may seem more vivid. Significantly, you may feel that you're starting to dream consciously, lucidly—that is, you're starting to know that you're dreaming *while* you're dreaming. It's good to encourage this. As you get into bed, simply form the intention to remember your dreams, and then try to remember them when you first awake. You can even form the intention to make deliberate choices in your dreams, to take a hand in writing the script even as you play your role, so that you're still *in* the world of the dream but not completely *of* it.

Then, as you return to the world of waking, you may start to notice, in some subtle ways around the edges, that you're also in *that* world but not of it.

14. The Myth of Monkey Mind

Back in Chapter 2, I described conversations I've often had at social gatherings with people who don't meditate, explaining why they don't think they can. Here's one I sometimes have with people who *do* meditate, especially at the beginning of a workshop I'm going to lead.

MEDITATOR: "Oh, my monkey mind is so out of control. I don't think you can tame it."

ME: "You're right."

When I become king of the world (I'm available), the third thing I'll outlaw, after car alarms and margarine, will be the term *monkey mind*. This phrase, denoting a mind that jumps incessantly from thought to thought like a wild monkey, suggests a naughty, mischievous, feral creature—a Curious George minus the lovability—that needs to be forcibly trapped and caged. This may be the single biggest, most damaging, most counterproductive notion in the field. Let's take this sucker down.

I can't tame your monkey mind. No one can tame your monkey mind, because there *is* no monkey mind.

First, for what it's worth, the Buddha never used this phrase, despite what some people will tell you. (Some websites too. The Buddha is right up there with Einstein, Lincoln, Mark Twain, and the Dalai Lama in the bogus-online-quote department.) Completely absent from the Sutras that record the Buddha's teachings, *monkey mind* or *mind monkey* was coined by Chinese writers some eight hundred years after his death. But more important than its origin is its insinuation that the presence of thoughts, in meditation or in life, is a big problem requiring harsh measures.

It isn't.

You've heard that from me already, and hopefully you've confirmed it in your own experience. But people often have trouble hearing it. (What's the aural equivalent of a blind spot?) More than once, a student who's heard his teacher say for months that thoughts don't matter has suddenly *gotten* it in meditation and then whined, "Why didn't you say so before?"

The idea that thoughts are problematic does arise from a right impulse, the rightest one there is: the instinctive desire for peace, for silence, for freedom. The mistake is the assumption that this silent inner freedom can't coexist with thinking. That's usually an unexamined assumption. Just a few minutes examining it, and it falls apart.

Monkeys are cute little critters. The monkey is not your enemy. In fact, the monkey may not even exist. Let's take a look at the alleged mind that's creating all this alleged trouble.

I'm speaking literally. *Look* at your mind.

Can you see it?

Can you find your mind? I'll wait. . . .

. . .

Where is the wild entity that supposedly does all this thinking? I'm not talking about the brain—the physical organ—and neither are the people who complain about their monkey mind. The brain doesn't jump around like a monkey; it sits at perfect rest within the cranium. (And in any event, we never experience the brain. We just have thoughts about it, usually based on what we half remember from some science class.) But where is the mind? You can locate the hand that picks up your fork; you can locate the foot that kicks the ball; you can locate the nose that sniffs the air; but where is the mind that thinks the thoughts?

This is not a merely rhetorical point. It's an experiential suggestion. Please try, in whatever way you can devise, to experience this mind, this thinker of thoughts.

. . .

No luck? Me neither. OK, then, let's try an analogy. We've all talked about the wind. *The wind blows.* Now, our language has subjects and verbs, to indicate two different entities: actor and action. *The boy runs. Boy* is the actor and *runs* is the action he performs. *Wind* is the actor and *blows* is the action it performs. But when the boy gets tired of running, he can take a time-out, sit down, enjoy a refreshing beverage, and we still see him sitting there. Where is the wind when it stops blowing?

That's right: it's nowhere. There *is* no entity, no doer separate from the doing; it's a linguistic fiction. What we call *wind* is none other than the activity of blowing. But by tagging it with a noun, we've tarted it up as a thing. This conjuring up of things where they don't exist is called *reification*, literally "thingification." In the case of the wind, if it blows really hard we reify it further, call it Hurricane Melvin, and listen to news commentators describe how Melvin has unleashed his fury on the Dominican Republic and has now set his sights on the Florida Keys.

Now please consider the possibility that mind is like wind. (Just turn the first letter upside down.) Apart from blowing, wind doesn't exist. Apart from thinking, mind doesn't exist; it's a product of reification.

There is no monkey.

And that's why this discussion is not just armchair philosophy: it has the most practical of bottom lines. When you set out to track the monkey, catch the monkey, tame the monkey, shock the monkey— whatever—you're doomed to failure. You will never, ever, *ever* catch a monkey that doesn't exist. You're chasing a ghost. The harder you chase it, the more reality you give it—the more convincingly you reify it. And that's good news. It means you can call off the expedition and relax. You've been chasing mental activity. And what is this "chasing" stuff? It's *more* mental activity. Activity has been chasing activity, like a dog chasing its tail. There's nothing to do now but have a good laugh.

Of course, we can object that, even if there's no separate mind to think thoughts, that solves nothing. Whether they're thoughts about cooking dinner or thoughts about chasing thoughts, those pesky thoughts are still there. We couldn't find the mind, but thoughts still find us. Mind may be insubstantial, but thoughts are all *too* substantial.

Well, are they now? (*Now* we take off the gloves.) Here's another experiential suggestion:

Please sit back, close your eyes, let things settle for a moment or two. Then pick the next thought that comes along, and take a look at it.

Where does it start?

Where does it end?

How much room does it take up?

How much space is around it?

What divides it from the next thought?

Does it hold still for your examination?

Let's say the thought is about a rock. Is the thought heavy like a rock? Or if it's about thunder, is it loud like thunder? What *is* it like?

Can you really say that this is *a* thought? Is it a single, bright pinpoint of thinking, like a star, or is it like a constellation of stars, some dimmer and some brighter? If it's like a constellation, is its form stable or shifting? Are the spaces between the stars clear, or blurred and mushed by a lot of interstellar dust?

If your thought is about, say, the Three Stooges, there might be a constellation of images and impressions of Larry, Moe, and Curly together; Larry separately; Moe separately; Curly separately; Curly's lame replacements (Shemp, Curly Joe, Joe Besser) dodging in and out around the periphery; your own love or loathing of the Stooges' antics; and so forth. How many thoughts is that? Can you isolate any one of them as a single, starlike data point? Or does it also break down in turn?

Take your time. Really look. For all these years, thoughts have dominated your life. It might be important to spend a few minutes seeing what they are.

As you're examining the thought about (say) the rock, are you really still having a thought about a rock, in just the same way as when the thought first, spontaneously arose? Or has the thought about the rock been replaced by a thought about the thought about the rock?

Does this mean that the moment we actually *look* at a thought, *that* thought is not quite there anymore?

Under this kind of scrutiny, it doesn't take long for these thought thingies that seemed so solid to start breaking down. The closer we look at them, the emptier they appear. If we had to describe them, we might be tempted to say they're a flux where there's nothing to fluctuate—a mesh of ripples on an ocean of nothin'. It turns out they're not solid, discrete, definable entities, like so many little marbles, but more like a shifting, shimmering light show.

Why haven't we noticed this before? Well, apparently we've never really looked at thoughts before. We've been too busy thinking. We've been too busy engaging in thoughts, and *in* is a key word here. We could say that thoughts are like travel brochures. There's a pile of them here on the table—one for Hawaii, one for Ireland, one for Australia—and we get so engaged in reading the text and looking at the pictures that it's as if we're *in* Hawaii or Ireland or Australia. We're so busy walking the streets of Dublin and choosing which pub to pop into that we forget we're in Cleveland, reading a brochure.

So, while we're busy thinking, we don't see the thought. When we try to look at it, it proves to be made of mist. But we *don't* look at it as long as we're either being seduced by it, which is what most people call life, or battling it, which is what most people call meditation.

It's really worthwhile pursuing this sort of inquiry for as long as it takes to become deeply convinced of the flimsy, bogus nature of all this mental activity that we once found so problematic. The mind is a ghost monkey, and its thoughts are ghost monkey business.

～

And therefore . . . what?

What do we do about these shifting, insubstantial thoughts?

Well, what does the ocean do about waves? What does the sky do about clouds? What does space do about galaxies?

Nothing.

The waves can toss all they want, and the ocean goes on resting in its bed. The clouds can rain or hail or blow away, and the sky remains equally skylike. Galaxies are created and destroyed over billions of years, and space is naturally, timelessly untouched, incorruptibly spacious.

You are not your thoughts. You are the spacelike awareness within which they frictionlessly come and go.

So . . . fuhgeddabouddit. You can treat thoughts as if they're in a language you don't understand. "I can't he-e-e-ear you!" All this time you've been playing Whac-a-Thought; now you can just drop your mallet and refuse to play. Let them pop their little heads up and down. So what?

"Sometimes in meditation I find myself thinking, 'If I could just figure out this one issue, resolve this one thought, my mind would be clear and then I could settle down.' "

Don't fall for it. Or what the hell, go ahead and try it. What you'll find is that (a) you probably *don't* work it out, and (b) it's soon replaced by *another* thought, and now you're sure that *this* is the one whose resolution will leave you at last with—ta-dah!—a clear mind. The Advaita sage Mooji sometimes asks, "What was your problem three problems ago?" In meditation, that question becomes, "What was your all-important, all-engrossing thought three all-important, all-engrossing thoughts ago?" And as the brilliant British teacher Rupert Spira has put it, "Don't worry about the mind being confused. Mind is always confused. There is no such thing as an unconfused mind."

"But sometimes I get so caught up in thoughts that I forget I'm supposed to be meditating."

That happens to everyone, especially early on. What to do about it? There's only one thing you *can* do about it: nothing. When you're caught up, you don't realize you're caught up, because you're caught up, so there's nothing you can do. The moment you realize you've *been* caught up, you're no longer caught up, because you've realized it, so there's nothing you *have* to do. Anything you try to do about it will be an attempt to travel back in time to three seconds ago and deal with the thought you were having then. This doesn't work.

Sometimes you'll get caught up over and over, and you'll set your jaw and try to come back to the mantra or heart center or whatever you're meditating on with extra-strength determination, to make sure that this time you *stay* there for three minutes—or even three seconds, for God's sake—into the future. This doesn't work either.

That's right: the situation is absurd. Naturally, you'll try to come up with clever strategies to work around the absurdity. Those strategies are what's known as . . . thoughts. The thought "Maybe I can strategize my way out of these thoughts" is a thought. The thought "These thoughts are a problem that requires a strategy" is a thought. Sadly, your cleverest thought can't help you. Happily, your dumbest thought can't hurt you. Increasingly, you can't tell the clever ones from the dumb ones. Eventually, you'll give up on all these shenanigans and realize that, unbelievably, thoughts don't take you away from anything, don't interfere with anything. How much distance lies between your thought and the peace, the silent awareness that you seek? Zero. The thoughts arise *within* silent awareness—in fact, as we saw in Chapter 9, they're made out of silent awareness, as the ripples are made of lake. Thoughts don't matter unless you give them that power, and you can withdraw that power in any instant, *this* instant.

If you get nothing else from this book, this might be the thing to get:

Just.

Ignore.

Thoughts.

Not silence them, not annihilate them, not resolve them, but ignore them. Whether you're sitting in "meditation" or just living your life, you're not at their mercy. You can ignore them. How? *Just freaking ignore them!*

You know exactly how to do this because you've done it with people. From time to time we all find ourselves having to listen to—or at least pretend to listen to—someone who insists on telling us a long, involved, convoluted, multicharacter, sometimes very dramatic, never very interesting story. There are usually a lot of *so-then-she-said*'s and *so-then-I-said*'s. It may verge on sheer fantasy, what in Yiddish is called a *bubbe maiseh*, a "granny story," with the (rather ungallant) implication that Bubby yammers on and on with tales that are not to be taken seriously. But we love Bubby, so we smile and nod, perhaps throw in an occasional "Really?" or "You don't say!" and let everything go softly out of focus. We don't argue with her. We don't push her out of the house. We don't duct-tape her mouth shut. We just let her talk, which she's going to do whether we "let" her or not. But we don't really listen.

Why be harsher on yourself—or, rather, your mind—than you are on Bubby? As long as you have a mind, or at least a bunch of shimmering thinking, you may as well love it. Consider the mind just one more dear, wacky, beleaguered friend. You don't have to fix it, you don't have to silence it. Just don't buy into its bubbe maiseh.

And actually, that poor, maligned monkey—that is, the thought activity that we call the monkey—is more accommodating than Bubby. All this time that it's been monkeying around, swinging from branch to branch, it hasn't been swinging aimlessly. Like the mouse under Ganesha's oozing dessert bowl, it's just looking for a treat—the bliss at the core of our being. As soon it smells that banana, it starts to settle down. We just have to spend enough time hanging out in that vicinity, exposing ourselves to the process, and the gravity of bliss takes over, pulling us naturally toward silence.

All this time, we've had it backward. We thought we'd find serenity by quieting our thoughts, but our thoughts quiet themselves as we sink into serenity—it's a side effect. And by then it doesn't matter, because we're already serene.

> *Therefore I do not run like someone running aimlessly; I do not fight like a boxer beating the air.*
>
> —1 CORINTHIANS 9:26

~

Three words: just ignore thoughts.

If you can deeply hear this, it may be all the meditation instruction you'll ever need. I'm very serious about this. In fact, for your next sitting session, I would suggest the following:

As usual, sit, close your eyes, loosen up, breathe—whatever preparation is helpful to you. Then just ignore thoughts.

"But that's not meditation."

The thought "That's not meditation" is a thought—ignore it.

"But how do I ignore thoughts?"

That's a thought—ignore it.

"But—"

That's a thought—ignore it.

"Wait . . . oh, I think I get it. Hey, this is cool."

That's a thought—ignore it.

Thoughts, we could say, are like snowflakes falling outside your window, giving the neighborhood a picturesque dusting. You can spend the whole day and night sticking your hand out the window, trying to catch them or count them or bat them away. Pretty soon you find yourself wondering, "Wait, how'd all this snow get in my room? Better grab my shovel and start digging. That'll keep me nice and busy. . . ."

Or you can just close the window, stay cozy, and let it snow, let it snow, let it snow.

15. *Meditating on Self and Other*

You're walking down the street. Maybe you're wearing new shoes and they're a little tight. *(Hmmm, should have gone half a size bigger.)* Your throat feels OK now. *(Guess I'm probably not catching a cold after all.)* You're thinking about a project you have to finish, or the movie you're going to see tonight. *(That comment Fred made at the office better not have been a spoiler.)* Occasionally your thoughts go to longer-term concerns about finances or family or health, with flashes of mild or intense emotions connected with them. The drama of which you're always at the center—your life, as you call it—is keeping on keeping on.

Meanwhile, you pass houses and buildings, perhaps dozens or even hundreds of them, but they glide through the periphery of your attention, barely noticed—just backdrops to your drama. They're like the flat, two-dimensional false fronts on movie sets. It may not register on you that those buildings are full of people, all of them as real as you are, all as engaged in their own life dramas as you are in yours, all with hopes and fears for themselves and their families that are as urgent to them as yours are to you. And when they walk past *your* house, to them it's just a flat backdrop.

Or you're driving to work and running late. The focus of your drama at the moment (your motivation, as actors call it) is getting to work on time. In the background there may be echoes of the grumpy, coffee-hasn't-kicked-in-yet conversation you had with your spouse over breakfast. Meanwhile, you deal with hundreds of other cars. Some are obstacles to your speedy commute, which you need to navigate your way around, and some are not. Period. It doesn't occur to you that each is occupied by a driver whose drama is as rich and as intensely felt as yours. That guy who just cut you off may be speeding to his mother's deathbed.

How strange! Seven billion people on this planet, and one of them—the one I call "I"—is so much more important and real than all the others. There's a striking inequality here, a lopsidedness. Imagine an old-fashioned balance scale. You sit down in one pan, and then watch as the other seven billion people crowd into the other pan and jostle for seats. Which side of the scale goes down?

Usually when people use the word *I*, they're referring to one of two things. One is the mind, which, as we've seen, is really a name for our shifting light show of mental activity. "I'm a liberal." "I'm a conservative." "I'm bewildered." "I'm right." "I'm praying for rain." "I'm waiting for Christmas." The other is the body. "I'm eating." "I'm tired." "I'm over here, behind the tree." "I look like Bill Murray." But now, through our deepening meditative experience and insight, we've been finding that our identification with the mind is less rigidly fixed than it once was. Could that be true of our identification with the body as well?

A sage was once asked about dying, and he said, "It's like taking off a tight shoe." But you don't have to wait for death: through the practices you've been doing, the tight-shoe relationship with the body is loosening up already. That's very natural. People in moments of being "in the zone" while playing sports or performing onstage or trading stocks often notice that the sense of in-the-body-ness somehow thins out or even evaporates. When I taught English and the kids and I got into a great session, with fresh insights flowing in a stream of collaborative discovery like jazz players when they're really cooking, I would sometimes look over, notice my body reflected in the window, and think, "What's *that* thing?!" Meditation is a way of starting to live our lives in that zone, where the body, in a way that's hard to explain but effortlessly experienced, is just a footnote.

A third definition of *I*, which also has a limiting, tight-shoe nature and which is also loosening up, is the sense of being a *self*—that is, self with a small *s*, a separate self, an ego, a person. Even before we first learned that "There's no 'I' in team," we were attracted to the possibility of being part of something bigger than our individual egos. Without being told, we know that there's something fine and noble about giving up our preoccupation with personal self, losing it in the larger identity of team or family, nation or world.

And when we try it, we discover that it's not only noble: *it feels good*. After all our scurrying about, hoarding and protecting our precious little cup of self-interest, worrying that we might spill a drop here or there, it's a *relief* to pour it into the collective ocean. Our movie villains, from Dr. No to Dr. Evil, embody that selfishness, often with a soupçon of perverty erotic narcissism: there's something cramped and twisted about being caught up in me, me, me. Our heroes embody the opposite impulse. When Braveheart gives up his life for freedom, or Rick makes Ilsa get on the plane out of Casablanca, we don't pity them. We admire and envy them; we vicariously sense how freeing it might be to escape the straitjacket of self.

> As the "I" disappears, that which remains to witness the disappearance of "I"—that is pure, timeless joy.
>
> —MOOJI

Hundreds of years ago, Tibetan lamas devised ingenious meditative practices for escaping this straitjacket.

∼

Please sit in your preferred position, close your eyes, and do a few minutes of conscious breathing (pranayama) or whatever helps you to naturally settle.

Now think of an acquaintance—someone you know fairly well but have no very strong feelings about, either positive or negative. A neighbor, classmate, or colleague is fine. Imagine that this person is present, as if sitting right in front of you. Let's call her Lois. It's not important to visualize Lois clearly. Just have the thought of her being there in front of you, the feeling of her presence.

Note your sense of yourself, the one who's sitting on the chair or cushion and meditating. *Me*, the small-*s* self . . . just our usual, lifelong sense of ourselves at the center of things, the one to whom all experience is happening, the one who at any given moment might be warm or cool, happy or sad.

There's no judgment here. It's very normal that this I or me—let's say my name is Lowell—perceives Lowell as the focal point, the hub of all experience, the one by whom sights are seen, sounds heard, emotions felt. He's the only one whose happiness I directly experience, and thus the one whose happiness *matters*. Even without any exaggerated ego-*tism*, it makes sense that this ordinary sense of being an ego, a separate self, makes me the most important thing there is . . . to me. Just as we learned from our grammar book, *I* is the first person.

Now note your sense of Lois. Note the perfectly ordinary sense of her as *other* than you, as someone "out there" on the other side of your skull bone and therefore less important. She's a third person, a *her*, or at best a second, a *you*. I am central, she is peripheral. I am self, she is other.

Notice also what the sense of selfness and the sense of otherness *feel* like. They're not just abstract ideas. Each has a different subtle texture or flavor that's distinct from the other.

Now switch the two.

That is, shift the sense of being the self, the center of everything, to Lois; shift the sense of being other, on the periphery, to Lowell.

This doesn't mean to try to see through Lois's eyes or read her mind. It doesn't mean to visualize Lois sitting in your chair or to imagine your-self inside her skin. It simply means that the flavor or texture of self, the prime status of first person, is now conferred upon Lois. Throw your selfness to her, like a ventriloquist throwing his voice. She's now the important one, the hub of all experience, while Lowell, the one sitting in your chair, has taken on that other flavor and is left as just another peripheral person. It's as if you've both been wearing those stick-on name tags that you get at workshops and conventions: "Hello! My name is: Self." "Hello! My name is: Other." Just switch the name tags.

And now just stay there. Abide there. Marinate in that situation, letting Lois be the center of the world just as Lowell was for so many years. Let Lowell languish in the shadows, practically forgotten.

Doing just this much is plenty for now. After a lifetime of identifying with an ego, giving it away even for a few minutes can be challenging. Then let the whole Lois-and-Lowell situation dissolve, and sit for a while in the space that remains. Come out slowly.

~

If you feel you've successfully made the self-and-other shift, in subsequent sessions you can take this practice further. Start as before, make the self-and-other shift, and then try giving things to Lois. Give her Lowell's car. Give her his house. Give her his computer, with all the precious poems and spreadsheets and vacation photos he's carefully stored on his hard drive. Wow! Give her all his proudest achievements: the athletic records he set in high school, the accolades he's earned in his profession. Employee of the month! Emmy nomination! Cool! Give her all the credit. Empty out Lowell's bank account—in cash—and pour it all onto Lois as she joyfully showers in it. Yee-ha! If you've really made the switch of self and other, Lowell is now just another person, a third-person *he*, half-forgotten in the shadows, while Lois is *I*, so heaping all these boons on Lois will feel *good*. You may find yourself smiling broadly.

Once you've thoroughly showered I-Lois with bounty, you can try doing this with additional people. In a single session, you might use one person or a few. Summon the person's presence, switch the status of self and other, and give the new self all your stuff. That is, give the old self's (Lowell's) stuff to the new I (whoever). Keep nothing for Lowell— clean him out.

At first, stick with "neutral" people, those who don't provoke intense feelings and with whom your relationships are simple. That way, the practice doesn't run into the complications of shared history and tangled feelings. In later sessions, you can move on to people you're closer to, whom you like or love. If thoughts about your interpersonal drama come up, just treat them like any other thoughts: don't suppress them, don't engage with them, disregard them. Keep it simple.

Then, if you continue to feel that this kind of practice has juice in it for you, the next step is to use as the other person someone you resent, fear, dislike, or even hate. If you're lucky enough not to have anyone like that in your personal life, you can choose someone from the worlds of media or politics, where (sadly) there never seems to be a shortage of the easy-to-loathe. Naturally, this can be more challenging. If you've worked your way up to using your ex or your abusive parent or the politician you think has destroyed your country, a lot of intensely felt content is apt to come up. Again, recognize all this as just thought and disregard it—this is not the time for psychotherapy. Keep your focus on the simple, radical act of conferring the status of self on another person, and the status of just-another-person on yourself.

You can also go beyond individuals and try giving your status of selfness to groups of people, such as your nuclear family, then your extended family, then, say, all victims of war, all abused animals, and eventually all sentient beings. But only do this if you can keep your sense of the group real and concrete, as you did with individuals: don't let it become just an abstract or sentimental idea.

There's also an advanced form of this practice in which, rather than diverting heaps of money and glory from Lowell to Lois, you divert heaps of misery from Lois to Lowell. This can be tricky, and is best done with the guidance of a live teacher. But it's exciting to know that it's possible, and that there are people in this world who practice like that every day for all sentient beings—including you.

~

If we step back and look at what we've been doing here, it's really quite remarkable. We've spent a lifetime hoping that all the good stuff—all of life's winning lottery tickets—will land on our heads, and the losing tickets will land on others. But now we sit, give away all the good stuff, *and enjoy it!* There's no feeling of martyrdom or "self-sacrifice" in the usual sense of the word. If there is, go back to the beginning—it's an indication that you haven't successfully made the exchange of self and other.

Of course, the point of this practice is not to stop being Lowell and start being Lois, to trade in an old ego for a new one. It's to discover that you're not stuck in any ego at all, and that in coming unstuck there is deep joy and the end of our imagined isolation.

> All that is known is experience, but there is no independent self that experiences and no independent object, other, or world that is experienced. There is just the experiencing of experience.
>
> —RUPERT SPIRA

There are ways to extend this practice into daily life. Say you're standing in a long line at the post office, and at the head of the line is an elderly lady who's doing everything very, very s-l-o-w-l-y: deciding which stamp to buy for each letter, getting confused about the price, fishing in her pocketbook for money, and finally paying with carefully counted-out nickels and pennies. You can stay good and busy tormenting yourself by watching every move she makes, rolling your eyes with exasperation, clenching your jaw, trying to *will* her to move faster. That is, you can keep on doing what you've always done, and get the result you've always gotten—frustration—along with everyone else in line. Or you can make the switch. Let the old lady be the self, the center of everything, luxuriously taking her sweet time to conduct her business, while you're just another person in line, anonymous and inconsequential. If you can really do this, the effect is miraculous—you're liberated from your torment.

Pick people out of the crowd while you're walking through the mall or waiting in the airport, pick fellow motorists or subway riders while you're commuting, and for a few moments let them be the center of the universe instead of you. These simple experiences, like that little sample spoonful of raspberry sorbet they give you at the ice cream counter, is a foretaste of the perks of *total* freedom from ego. That's where you're headed. (*New Yorker* cartoon: a bunch of penguins milling around on an ice floe. Caption: "Which one is me?")

In my teaching days, as much as I loved being in the classroom with the kids, I hated faculty meetings. I would sit in the back of the room with the other faculty bad boys, groaning as one speaker after another got his moment in the sun, took the floor, and bloviated away for ten endless minutes to say something I could have read in a thirty-second memo. Then I learned this technique and started making the switch, so that it was "my" moment in the sun. Problem solved: tedium converted to enlightenment practice.

I first trained in this kind of self-and-other meditation some twenty years ago with Charles Genoud, a brilliant Buddhist teacher from Switzerland. He has focused on this approach for decades, and it shows. His presence somehow seems both lighter than air and solid, grounded as a rock, and he speaks a soft, French-accented English in which the word *other* sounds like "awe-there." I can still hear him saying,

> Self and awe-there are like *here* and *there*. Everyone agrees there is a "here," but everyone disagrees about where it is. I think it is right here. You think it is over there. In the same way, everyone agrees that there is a self, but everyone disagrees about who it is. It seems obvious to me that I am the self, but you insist that it is you. It is a point of view—a perspective.

The moment we relax our grip on that perspective, life lightens up. At the red light you can stop feeling stuck, if you can let go of being the self who's *here* and participate in the joy of the others *there* on the cross street, happily driving through their green light.

This doesn't mean you dissolve into some kind of bland, generic, impersonal mush, that you no longer create and contribute to society in your unique way. It means that the old preoccupation with self gets out of the way of your creating and contributing.

~

What I've presented in this chapter thus far is essentially Charles's version of the medieval Tibetan technique of *tonglen*, which he insightfully adapted to address some of the psychological realities of modern life. In time, I found myself developing a modern adaptation of my own, one that takes advantage of our heavy exposure to entertainment media. The idea came while I was writing *Cinema Nirvana*, my book about unintended enlightenment lessons in movies like *Jaws* and *Snow White and the Seven Dwarfs*.

I realized that, when we take our seat in a theater and the lights go down, something extraordinary happens. We lose sight of "ourselves"—our bodies, that is—and focus on Scarlett Johansson instead. This is one of the reasons why watching movies on TV in a well-lit living room doesn't have the same power. We need to *identify* with the central character—that is, shift our sense of self to him or her, while our old self becomes just another person, one more anonymous member of the audience, *literally* languishing in the shadows.

We know perfectly well that we're seeing mere two-dimensional representations of a fictional character, portrayed by an actor who's paid to recite lines from a script, with several days or years of the character's life weirdly condensed into two hours. We know that the bombs she dodges are products of pyrotechnics professionals and the sound effects department, and that the man she kisses is an actor who kissed someone else in his last film. Yet when Scarlett's in danger, our heart pounds; when she's in love, our heart swells. This is not possible unless we've stopped identifying as audience member Joe Shmoe and identified instead with the fabricated hero. Moviegoing as you've done it all your life is already an exercise in melting out of your identification with ego, the isolated self. This is part of what makes moviegoing, in its best moments, a sublime, transcendent experience.

There are standard cinematic techniques that make sure we know who the star is. The star gets the most screen time. She gets a lot of close-ups, especially at moments of high stress or deep feeling, which bring us inside her emotional world, make us feel as if we're inside her skin, make her the first person—the film's "I." She usually has a highly symmetrical, unblemished, unlined face, whose beauty is almost a blankness, like our invisible self, the *here* from which we look out at the world. Like her face, her body must approach the abstract, Platonic, Greek-sculpture ideal of the human form.

There are also supporting characters, including perhaps the lead character's spouse or lover, best friend or confidant, or perhaps an antagonist. They get occasional close-ups, but far fewer than the lead. They're often shown in medium shot, sharing the frame with the star or one or two others. We feel some involvement with them, but not the heavy emotional investment we have in the star. We just don't care about them as much. They're defined by their relationship with the central character; without it, they wouldn't be in the film. They're like planets orbiting around the star. Since they represent *there*, the visible others outside our self, they can include character actors whose faces have more lines and asymmetry—more character. Their bodies can be fat or thin, short or tall, like those of actual humans.

Finally, there are bit characters, walk-ons, extras. They're like distant asteroids in the outer reaches of the star's solar system, or comets that flash by briefly. They may have one or two lines or none. They make a wisecrack as they bag the star's groceries or wash the star's car, and then we forget about them. They may be the thousands of soldiers in the hero's army, or the thousands of panicked victims fleeing from Godzilla. They're pretty much expendable and interchangeable. We don't care about them. (And these days they may be products of CGI anyway.)

Now, then . . .

Please imagine a movie about *your* life, a movie in which you're the central character. Recall it as if you saw it in a theater last night. Certain key scenes of great challenge or emotion probably come right to mind . . . and there you are, in close-up because you're the star, going through it all. Naturally, you can feel those emotions clearly, and you care deeply about those challenges.

And there are the handful of major supporting characters: perhaps your spouse or partner, your parents or children, with their occasional close-ups and more frequent medium shots, often shared with you. Their importance, their "major" status, derives from their closeness to *you*; they are "supporting" characters because they prop up the circumstances of *your* life. To some degree you feel their pain and their joy, but not the way you feel yours.

And then there are the extras, bagging your groceries or washing your car, whose names you may not even know. It rarely occurs to you that they have homes and challenges and inner lives of their own. They're interchangeable.

Now let that movie fade to black: The End.

And now please imagine that you saw a different movie last night, about one of your supporting characters. Only, since this is her movie, now *she's* the star. She gets the most screen time, she gets the close-ups, her challenges and triumphs define the story arc. When you sit in the dark and watch this film, you identify with *her*, laughing or crying when she rises in triumph or goes down in defeat. Her various supporting characters come and go: this one, that one, and—oh hey, there's you, filling out a medium shot. You care about those supporting characters some, but only as they relate to the star.

Now let *that* movie fade to black.

And now please imagine yet another movie, one in which the guy who bags your groceries or washes your car is the star. You don't know much about his life, so you'll have to imagine it. There he is, waking up in bed, and—wow, look at that! He lives in a house! He has a wife! (His first supporting character.) Maybe his daughter doesn't feel well and wants to stay home from school. Maybe he has a favorite kind of music he listens to while he drives to work, or maybe he rides in a crowded bus. Where I live, he's probably Latino and may speak little or no English. Maybe he gets along well or poorly with his boss at the carwash (another supporting character). And here come the extras: people driving in to get their cars washed. Who knows what their names are? Who cares what jobs they drive off to? They don't even speak Spanish. Oh, and that one is you, with five seconds of screen time. You give him a pretty nice tip (or you don't), you drive off, and you're forgotten. His wife texts him: their daughter is really sick and needs to go to the hospital. And so on.

Fade to black.

~

Just reading this, just imagining like this, you may feel some erosion of your ego's centrality, its exclusive claim as the *here* perspective that leaves everyone else out *there*. And you may feel some corresponding taste of liberation. Being the center of the universe is a big job. Finding out you're just another person is a big relief.

You can get creative and invent your own approaches to softening up the small self's (imaginary) hard shell and sharing the central, starring role with others. One simple one that I like is the Rastafari expression *I and I*, used in place of *we*. To my ear, it has a nice, warm way of welcoming the second person in, or letting the first person out, to a more open, freely shared space, where there's *no* first or second. I and I will eat supper now. I and I will walk by the sea. I and I have come to a clearer understanding (or *over*standing, as they say). I and I have had a lovely day. I and I *love* I and I.

16. Retreating Forward

Go all the way with it. Do not back off. For once,
go all the goddamn way with what matters.

—ERNEST HEMINGWAY

At some point you may want to take Hemingway's advice, dive in, and for once go all the way into your meditative practice—at least for a weekend. That's what retreats are for.

Before the time of the Buddha, there were homeless *sadhus* (holy men) in India who dedicated their lives to solitary meditative practice. But when the Buddha attracted hundreds of full-time followers, he developed the idea of a monastic brotherhood that practiced together and moved as a group from place to place. They camped under trees and in caves, near the outskirts of towns and villages, so that they could come into town to beg food from the locals and, in return, provide spiritual instruction. But during the three-month monsoon season, moving about was difficult and there was the danger of trampling young rice plants, so the Buddha instituted the idea of a retreat. Some patron would provide shelter for him and his monks (and, later, nuns), and there they would devote their days to long hours of meditating and deepening their insight.

Today, retreats may be shorter or longer than three months and are not necessarily Buddhist. (Nor was the Buddha a Buddhist, by the way.)

(Nor was Christ a Christian.) But the essential idea is the same: you go somewhere remote from the bustle of daily life and thoroughly immerse yourself in extended sitting, usually several hours a day broken up into smaller chunks, under the supervision of an experienced teacher. Retreats can dramatically accelerate the enlightenment process. For that reason Maharishi refused to call them retreats—they were advances. I started attending them in my late teens, and my girlfriend at the time commented that every time I came back from one I was progressively more relaxed and my rough edges were more smoothed off. I was just a nicer person.

You may want to start with a shorter retreat, just a weekend or a week your first time out. There are many excellent teachers who lead retreats regularly, often internationally. I of course favor those who teach a natural, effortless approach to sitting and a nondual perspective (see Chapter 21). Three to whom I can personally give my highest rating are Adyashanti, Rupert Spira, and Mooji.

Retreats are great. There are typically two or three teaching sessions or guided meditations per day, your meals are provided, you have a nice little room or cabin or dorm, there are often beautiful grounds to walk around, and you're encouraged (or required) to unplug from your phone and other connections to the so-called real world.

On many retreats, there's no talking allowed outside of the teaching sessions.

Now, this is the point where many people say, "What? Keep silent for a whole weekend? I could *never* do that."

Ummm . . . why not?

Will you explode? Will you die or get pregnant? Is this talking thing so urgent or so fabulous that (assuming you live to be seventy-five) you have to talk for all 27,394 days of your life and can't spare two or three? Perhaps you've raised (or been) a child who insisted, "No, I won't try asparagus, I'll *never* like asparagus." The grown-ups know that someday that kid is gonna try asparagus and see what a delicious thing he's been missing all these years. That's how I feel about people who think they'll never enjoy silence. C'mon, Junior—give it a chance.

Silence is delicious. It's rejuvenating. It's a great gift to yourself. It restoreth the soul. Until you let go of talking for a little while, you have no idea how much energy it consumes. It's great to sit down every day to your silent lunch and, undistracted by the usual chitchat, deeply appreciate what it's like to taste your soup and to grind salad with your teeth so it can miraculously become your flesh. It's also instructive to hear all the stories your mind makes up about the other folks in the dining hall, and then find out on the last day, when everyone comes out of silence, how comically wrong you were about them. Unplugging from vocal chatter helps us hear how much mental chatter has been running underneath it . . . and then hear the silence underneath *that*. Language has texture, color, and boundaries, which makes it fascinating. Silence is textureless, colorless, and boundless, which makes it liberating.

But don't try this at home—at least, not at first. The process of emotional discharge we discussed earlier can sometimes be intense and confusing when you meditate long hours, and it requires the clear, stable presence of the teacher to point you through it. Later, after you've attended several supervised retreats and are familiar with their possible roller-coaster aspect, you can do short retreats on your own. Many cities have lovely monasteries and retreat centers close by where you can get an inexpensive room and meals for a few days and be left alone.

Sometimes people come home from a whirlwind vacation more exhausted than when they left, but this kind of weekend will truly rejuvenate you.

Oh, and one more thing: In case you're interested in meeting some really kind, balanced, cooled-out people, one of whom may turn out to be your life partner, don't go to bars—go on retreats. It wasn't my intention, but that's where I met both of my wives.

17. Meditating on Love

Please clasp your hands with the fingers laced together. This is a nice, comfy gesture that you've probably made thousands of times without ever thinking about it.

But now take a closer look. You have what we could call an upper hand and a lower hand. In the photo, my left hand is in the upper position; that is, my left thumb is at the top of the stack, and then the fingers alternate till my right pinky is at the bottom. This is the way I always do it. Please note which way *you* always do it.

Now do it the other way.

Ewwwwww!

Feels creepy, doesn't it? Just *wrong*.

Why is that? Is there an actual, structural difference between your two hands that makes one fit comfortably on top and the other not?

Nope. It's just habit. Physically, the hands pretty much mirror each other. What makes one arrangement feel "good" and the other "bad" is *conditioning.* The actual reality of our experience—of our hands or of anything else—is filtered through a web of mental habits, produced by such factors as education, social indoctrination, past associations, and, as in this case, simple familiarity or unfamiliarity. Beauty (and ugliness) are in the eye (or, rather, the mind) of the beholder. As Hamlet puts it,

> There is nothing either good or bad, but thinking makes it so.

Many people think all spiders are creepy-nasty-scary. Some of my neighbors will immediately squish any spider that shows up on their property—even if they know it's not a black widow, the only venomous species around here. Others find spiders benign or even beautiful. In both cases, pretty much the same image is falling on the retina. The raw sensory perception is about the same, but it's filtered through a different overlay of thought. One person can appreciate a thing's beauty where another judges it repulsive. If we're lucky, our appreciation widens. A few months ago I was getting ready to put a fresh coat of paint on our old fence, when Yaffa (my wife) pointed out how beautiful all the weathering and scuffs and nicks were. I took another look, and danged if it wasn't a work of art—our own backyard Rothko. I put the paint back in the storage shed and spent the afternoon making music. I've also found myself with a deepening appreciation of both gorgeous women *and* men, in a way that has nothing to do with any urge to copulate with them—as well as gorgeous mountains, stars, lakes, shoes, fire engines . . .

You may have noticed that people who are happier, more open, more relaxed—wise people, people who seem to have it together, people you might even go to for guidance in life—are generally not caught up in a lot of rigid judgment. Certainly they have their preferences, but they *know* that they're just preferences: they may prefer tea or jazz or the Red Sox, but they can see how other people might prefer coffee or techno or the Yankees without being evil or insane. It's as if their sense of appreciation has a wide-angle lens that allows space for the potential beauty of their whole perceptual environment.

This includes people. Those wise ones may prefer to hang with certain people, but they don't condemn the others. And they understand the psychologically astute biblical verse, "Judge not, that ye be not judged." Cutting other people slack leaves you slack for yourself. The wise ones don't say "Ewwwwww!" a lot. They do say "Wow!" a lot. Think of Jesus, Buddha, the Dalai Lama, Einstein, Yoda, Mister Rogers. It's hard to imagine any of them going into a tizzy because they think some spider or human they've encountered is repulsive or irredeemably awful. It's easy to imagine all of them deeply savoring the beauty and value of every being they encounter.

There's a name for this kind of appreciation: love.

Now, our culture has a long history of equating love with wild, crazy, sexually charged, narrowly fixated passion. And that kind of passion can certainly be an exciting and ultimately instructive part of our journey. But in our quieter, saner moments we know that love is something deeper and wider than that. When songs tell us that love stinks, love hurts, love bites, love is a losing game, or love will tear us apart, we know the topic is not really love but passion and attachment. Unlike passion and attachment, love is never a mistake. It never creates problems. We also know that the people we admire as embodying the highest values of life embody great love, and their example challenges us to do likewise. If we can really rise to that challenge, we can be more like them: happier, wiser, more relaxed, more wide-angle-lens appreciative . . . more enlightened.

Particularly in modern Western society, where it's common to have several serious romantic connections and breakups in a lifetime, many people go around with a lot of emotional damage—the walking wounded. For them it may be especially healing to learn how to keep the heart open, even as you're parting ways, even to those who've done you wrong.

But how to do that? I'll assume you're as allergic as I am to the sort of false, forced, surfacey, lovey-schmovey, paste-on-a-smiley-face-even-if-I-really-want-to-punch-your-lights-out approach that often passes for enlightenment or spirituality. In Robert Browning's hilarious, dark poem "Soliloquy of the Spanish Cloister," one monk spends most of his time in the monastery seething with hatred for another. In between reciting pious prayers to the Virgin Mary, he mutters, "Gr-r-r— you swine!" and plots various methods of tricking the guy into eternal damnation.

We don't have to be content with faking it. We can broaden our ability to love by using methods that skillfully apply the principles of natural meditation—simplicity, spontaneity, direct experience, natural gravitation toward the blissful. These methods exist in various forms in a number of traditions. The ones that I've found especially effective and accessible derive from the wisdom traditions of Tibet. For my instruction in them I am indebted to Dr. John Makransky, who is both a professor of Buddhism and comparative theology at Boston College and an esteemed Tibetan Buddhist meditation teacher.

These practices begin with the idea of a *benefactor*—someone who, for you personally, embodies wide-open love and appreciation, and the wish for all that is good for you. It might be the Buddha, the Blessed Virgin, or another spiritual exemplar. It might be your wonderful uncle or auntie or granny, your spouse, your child. It might be someone who would never use the word *love* with you: your camp counselor, your football coach, your tenth-grade English teacher, your colleague, your dog. When Mister Rogers accepted a Lifetime Achievement Emmy in 1997, he told the audience, "All of us have special ones who have loved us into being. Would you just take, along with me, ten seconds to think of the people who have helped you become who you are?"

So . . . please take a few moments right now and think of benefactors you've had in your life—those who have loved you into being, who have appreciated your preciousness, who have done the opposite of judging you as a creepy spider. You generally know who they are because it feels *good* to think of them: when they cross your mind, you get a warm, smiley feeling. (And by the way, what a wonderful thing to be—someone who makes others happy just by crossing their minds. *There's* something to aspire to.)

Just this exercise, of realizing who your benefactors have been, can be very powerful. It's worth taking some time with it. You may find that, once you get that ball rolling, it continues to roll. You might wake up tomorrow and say, "Oh yeah, I had that terrific kindergarten teacher who saw something special in me and really helped me blossom." "The old guy who works at the corner store always has such a nice smile—he's genuinely happy to see me." Especially in times when you feel you've been navigating alone through the dark, simply calling the benefactors to mind will help you realize that you've had many lighthouses along the way.

~

Before we meditate on giving wider love, we're going to meditate on receiving it.

Please sit, close your eyes, and settle.

Start with a few minutes of one of the simpler techniques, such as meditation on the breath or a sound or the heart center. Or just settle and let your awareness be naturally spacious.

Now, within the spaciousness of your awareness, please imagine one of your benefactors in the space above your head.

It's not important to visualize the benefactor clearly. As with the self-and-other practice, as soon as you think of her, her presence has been invoked. And it's natural if a warm, smiley feeling starts to spontaneously arise as you recognize what she embodies: her total appreciation of you, her pure vision of your essential goodness, her wish for only good to befall you . . . her love.

It feels good to be loved. (It's what everyone wants.) Allow yourself to *bask* in that feeling, to bathe in it.

In fact, now imagine that that love takes the form of a shower of brilliant light, streaming down from the benefactor and completely irradiating you. Let every cell of your body be completely bathed and cleansed by this brilliant, beautiful light of love streaming down from the benefactor.

If any parts of your body have pain or ailments, let them receive a special extra dose. Let the very parts that have seemed like obstacles to comfort and happiness become the portals for receiving this healing, purifying light of love. Completely relax into it . . . give yourself up to it.

Stay like this for as long as you like, then come out slowly.

That's plenty for now. You're learning at a deep level—in your bones, in your cells—what love is, what its healing power feels like. And you're learning it from the world's leading experts, the benefactors. You can practice like this for days or weeks. You can use different benefactors, or you may feel strongly to stay with one. If it feels natural to have a few benefactors above you at once, beaming down on you together, that's fine. But keep it simple—don't overthink it.

At times you may notice that your whole body seems to be melting, dissolving into the love light streaming from the benefactors. That's also fine.

After irradiating the body, you can deepen the practice further by letting the light penetrate into the web of thoughts called your mind—purifying it, healing it—and eventually allowing it to dissolve into the light.

Then let the light penetrate beyond the mind to the level of your feelings, including all your fear and anger . . . purifying, healing, dissolving.

And finally your ego, the core sense of being a separate self: let that dissolve as well, so that only light remains.

Come out slowly.

~

This practice often stirs up deep emotions. That's fine. In fact, it's great. Remember, our capacity for love is being expanded, so it makes sense that we may feel deeply moved. Keep a box of tissues close by.

When you feel ready to extend this approach, first start the session by practicing as above: settling down, invoking the benefactor's presence, feeling the love pouring down on you, receiving it deeply.

Then, in the space in front of you, imagine a friend, a pet, or anyone else you're fond of in a straightforward way that's not complicated by a lot of drama. Again, don't try to visualize clearly—just think of him and you automatically feel his presence.

Now, as the brilliant, healing, purifying light of love continues to stream down into you from your benefactor, let it also stream out from your heart center, out through the front of your chest, and bathe the person in front of you.

Let the light irradiate every cell of the recipient's body.

Let it penetrate his mind . . .

his feelings . . .

his ego . . .

purifying them and dissolving them into light.

Then give up the idea of the three of you—you, the benefactor, and the recipient—as separate entities.

Allow the three of you to dissolve together into the light, until brilliant light is all that's left. Just light everywhere, all-suffusing, with no direction and no source.

Stay like this for as long as you like.

Finally, let even the sense of light dissolve, and rest in what's left: the awareness-space in which the whole practice has been taking place.

Come out *very* slowly.

~

Whew. This is powerful stuff.

Please note the psychological brilliance of the way the practice is structured. First we learn to *receive* unconditional love. For some people this is the most challenging part, but it doesn't matter whether we feel worthy, whether we feel lovable and precious. The benefactors, with their more enlightened vision, see that we *are* worthy, and who are we to argue? Just the mechanical process of receiving their light puts us in the position of accepting their love. Then, by allowing their love to penetrate through the body to the deepest levels of our being, irradiating and dissolving everything that seems to make us a separate person, we experience how love goes beyond the personal to the universal, showing us that what *we* are goes beyond the personal to the universal.

Then we allow the love light to come through us and do all that for others. In this practice, as with the meditation on self and other, after starting with individuals in front of you, you can move on to groups. You can also start with people who are easy to bathe with love and then move on to the hard cases. Don't go straight to the murderers and torturers and tyrants, but it is good to get to them eventually.

In this way, we step up and become junior varsity benefactors ourselves, working out first in the little gym behind our closed eyes, getting in shape for the marathon task (the *joyful* marathon task) of shining love throughout the world. You don't have to say a word about it. Just be what you are, what the benefactors have *shown* you you are. And when you fall back into judging yourself or others as not worthy or not precious or not beautiful, you can lace your fingers together in the non-usual way to remind yourself that this judgment is just an old habit—one that does nothing but constrict your own heart and your own happiness. Then let that habit go.

This is not just a pipe dream. There *are* people like this. I once had the great privilege of interviewing Mister Rogers on the phone. Many people don't know that he was an ordained minister, although he never preached religion as such. His ministry was his years of producing television and writing songs that gently calmed children's fears ("You Can Never Go Down the Drain") and offered them unconditional love ("It's You I Like"). I was doing research on mentors, and Mister Rogers told me how his life's work had been inspired by a great theology professor he had at seminary, an eccentric character who used to chain-smoke through his lectures, occasionally setting off small wastebasket fires with his discarded cigarette butts. In wintertime, he would often take a walk and return without his overcoat because he had given it to some homeless person.

Over time, Mister Rogers noticed that the professor, despite his own brilliance, never criticized people but always found ways to make them right—even if he had to stretch—and then used that positivity to inspire them to reach higher. Finally Mister Rogers asked him how he had come to be that way. "It came to me while I was studying the gospels," he answered. "One day I realized that the opposite of fault-finding is love, and I would rather love."

Near the end of our talk, Mister Rogers somehow managed to turn the interview around and make it about me. He started telling me what a wonderful person I was and what a wonderful teacher I was, how I must have changed the lives of so many students. Suddenly I was crying. Through my tears, I realized that he wasn't just making something up to be nice. By receiving the light of clear, loving vision from his benefactor, the professor, he had seen the luminous, perfect being at his own core. Now he was streaming it to me and seeing the perfection at *my* core. And now I do my best to stream it to you.

Your turn.

As Jesus said, "Love one another, as I have loved you."

As the Grateful Dead sang, "Turn on your love light—let it shine."

18. Advanced Glimmers

Skeleton walks into a bar and says, "Gimme a beer . . . and a mop."

Hopefully, what you've been learning from this book has been sticking to your ribs better than beer sticks to a skeleton's. That's because it's not just book learning. With any topic, say fly-fishing, if it's merely theoretical it's not going to do you much good when you suddenly find yourself hip-deep in the stream. But if you've been practicing any of the methods presented here with some semblance of regularity, then you've got your waders on right, you're casting nicely, and by now you're hooking some fish.

So this seems like a good time to check in and take another look at the growing, increasingly real, decreasingly theoretical effects of meditation in your life. Again, everything here is based on my thoroughly subjective, anecdotal, unscientific observations gathered from a lifetime of practice and teaching. And once again, you're invited to *look*, to see whether this or that kind of thing is in fact happening for you even a little, and, if so, to lean with the Vespa . . . gently cooperate with the developments. If some of them don't sound familiar yet, that's OK. They may be around the next corner. Keep leaning.

Hopefully by now you've at least seen that natural meditation is a handy tool for releasing stress and sharpening your mind, and if that's all you're interested in, that's fine. But *I* know that it's also an opening into a dimension that is the most important discovery a human being can make. Perhaps you're starting to suspect the same thing. Those are the glimmers I want to explore.

∾

One evening, as I was out for a stroll on the beach, I saw a woman with a small dog, just out of puppyhood. I had never seen a dog behave like this. It was in a state that I can only describe as ecstatic canine amazement, and it was rapidly going through what looked like four-legged versions of moonwalking, breakdancing, thrashing, and krumping. When I stopped to ask the woman what was going on, she told me, "This is the first time he's ever been on sand." It was as if, after spending his whole life thus far on solid ground, the dog was suddenly discovering that his world was governed by new laws of physics—laws that are freer, looser, and way more fun.

This is something like what happens to us. Somehow, life is becoming freer, looser, less rigid, less constricted. We find that we can draw on a wider range of creative possibilities, less bound by our old thinking and our old history—by anything before this moment. Al Hirschfeld, the great caricaturist who was still breaking fresh artistic ground well into his nineties, once said, "I'm not at all limited because I don't know what I'm doing." He had what the Zen masters call "beginner's mind," the freedom from stale concepts and assumptions that keeps our approach ever fresh. Those we call geniuses—a Hirschfeld or an Einstein—

retain that freshness and can keep pulling surprising things out of it for a lifetime. Everyone tells us to think outside the box; not everyone does. (If they did, they'd come up with a replacement for that tired cliché.) But now, with perhaps a little leaning into it, fresh thinking arises more easily. Whether you're a musician or an engineer or a school administrator, you just *see* creative options that weren't there before.

Jesus talked about that beginner's-mind freshness as well, saying that, to enter the kingdom of heaven—his term for enlightenment—we must become like children. I assume that he and the Buddha were very much like the most enlightened people I've been around, such as Mooji and the Dalai Lama. If so, they knew how to relax into childlike (not child*ish*) playfulness, and they loved to laugh. We can't blame them for the solemn portraits drawn later on by people who never met them.

This freshness may even be reflected in our physical aspect. You've probably seen people come home from vacation looking younger. Now you're taking a deeply rejuvenating vacation every day: vacating on the deepest level, marinating in vacancy. There are no guarantees, but you may find your friends telling you that, instead of aging, you're youthening. (Moisturizing regularly is also recommended.)

You may start to wonder if you're getting lazy—it may feel as if you're not *doing* anything. Yet, if you look objectively, you see that somehow everything's getting done. (I have no idea how this book is getting written.) It's not the doing that's going away, it's the doer—the sense of a separate self that has to work at interacting with separate objects. As that sense gradually evaporates, what's left is freedom. Before, life could seem like a big pot of some thick, sticky, highly viscous fluid we struggled to stir—maybe glue or tar or molasses. But now its viscosity has started to lessen. One day, it becomes infinitely nonviscous.

You may also find that you have more energy. There are neurochemical explanations for how this happens, but I like the story told by meditation teacher and former monk Peter Fenner:

> A swami in India was once asked by a student about the phenomenal level of his energy. "You hardly sleep," she said. "Where does this boundless flow of energy come from?"
>
> "Just imagine," he replied, "how much energy you would have if you didn't worry, or complain, or judge, or defend, or resist!"

Another consequence of this freshness is that you don't have to work as hard to have a good time. On Friday and Saturday nights (and now Thursday, the new Friday), my town's Main Street becomes a major bar scene. Yaffa and I will sometimes take a late-night walk through the middle of the action, just to enjoy the show: the clusters of young girls in their LBDs (little black dresses) and bare shoulders no matter how cold the air, hobbling up the sidewalk in their six-inch heels like novice stilt walkers . . . the guys in crisp button-downs or schlumpy T-shirts or leather jackets . . . all dodging and pursuing each other to the next club full of pounding music, drinking the next drink, smoking the next cigarette, sending the next text, all the while trying their hardest to be sexy and cool.

Not that there's anything wrong with that. It just seems like a whole lot of work. Sure, it's an expression of the restless energy of being twenty-something, but it's also just a louder, crasser form of what most of us continue to do as we get older: hobbling along on our own stilts in pursuit of the next big promotion or great restaurant or fabulous movie or cool gadget, or checking for the next allegedly life-changing post or tweet or system update. We've been at this since we were kids waiting for Christmas, always on the brink of opening the next present, the one that'll be so fantastic it'll make our heads explode with happiness.

There's nothing wrong with Christmas or movies or restaurants either. The question is, how long will it take us to figure out that there's no actual happiness content in any of these objects of experience? Break open the most delicious dark chocolate bar or the most amazing new iGadget in the world, and inside you'll find cocoa and sugar or resistors and circuit boards, but you won't find any happiness. The happiness comes from *us*, the awareness that experiences all the stuff. When you break open your awareness, you *do* find happiness—that's called meditation. And that is the best of news, because the external stuff is always changing and unstable. Your favorite restaurant suddenly goes downhill, your favorite TV show is canceled, your favorite shirt goes threadbare, even your infatuation with your favorite singer or novelist may go stale. It's pretty much guaranteed that your drinking capacity and your ability to hook up with desirable girls or guys eventually diminishes.

> *Well, my friends are gone and my hair is grey.*
> *I ache in the places where I used to play....*
> —LEONARD COHEN

If, like most people, you've been slaking your thirst by going about, trying to sip the happiness from all the ephemeral experiences, like a thirsty person trying to sip the dewdrops from the blades of grass before they evaporate in the morning sun, it's an endless and ultimately frustrating task. But now you're beginning to discover that the core of your own being is a brimming reservoir. That changes everything. It makes the dewdrops optional. If you *like* doing x, and you can do it without harming others, then no problem, God bless. But more and more, you don't *need* to do x, y, z, or anything else to be happy. You're happy just being. You're free. You can live your life. You can watch the next miniseries, race the next motorcycle, or, for that matter, party your way through every bar on Main Street, if you still want to. But gradually (and in a few cases suddenly), everything you do becomes an *expression* of happiness rather than a quest for it.

You may not look especially different. You're still you, but you see how to be you gracefully, without breaking the furniture. If, say, you're a witty, gossipy schmoozer, you tend to remain a witty, gossipy schmoozer. But if your gossip has had a mean-spirited edge to it or your schmoozing has been driven by a compulsive craving for attention, those tendencies will probably drain out. Your most obnoxious traits, the ones that cause the most discomfort for you and those close to you, start to wither. Eventually they become like old weeds deprived of water, dried-out mummies of their former selves that no longer compete for soil and nutrition with the healthy, desirable plants.

One trait that tends to fall away is the infatuation with victimhood narratives. (They're so boring.) You may know people who preface any story of bad luck with the phrase *of course*. "Of course, when *I* got to the front of the line, the clerk went on her lunch break." "Of course, when the day for *our* picnic came, it rained." No. It's not of course. You're not so special that the universe has made a point of setting its course to wreck your fun. You just ran into some bad luck . . . sort of like everybody else. Now, with our growing clarity and freshness, we start to see that our sense of victimhood was just a mental habit, one that we feel lighter and freer without—and we let it go. We see that we're not the target; we stop taking life personally. We've been asking the universe, as De Niro asks the mirror in *Taxi Driver*, "Are you talking to *me*?" Turns out the answer is no.

Other such habits fall away as well. Maybe you know someone who keeps having the same disastrous relationship again and again, only with different partners. Maybe that someone is you. If so, the whole melodrama has probably been driven by some notion you've been harboring, perhaps reducible to a single sentence like, "I need you to affirm me every day as the center of your world," or, "You're perfect. Let me fix you," or, "I know you'll desert me when I need you most," or, "I'm such an unlovable schmuck—I dare you to love me." I've seen people go through years of therapy and fail to see the pattern, even though, to their friends, it's as if they're walking around with it printed on their shirt. Even if they see it, they may hang on, as if they don't know how to let it go. But now, as we practice letting go of *every*thing for a few minutes a day, we start finding that we can let go of *any*thing.

This includes all kinds of useless worries and concerns. Perhaps Andy Warhol said it best:

Sometimes people let the same problem make them miserable for years when they could just say, "So what." That's one of my favorite things to say. "So what." . . . I don't know how I made it through all the years before I learned how to do that trick. It took a long time for me to learn it, but once you do, you never forget.

Challenging circumstances will still arise, whether they're breakups or health emergencies or professional crises or the deaths of loved ones. Those are the times when some people will throw up their hands and say, "How can I meditate with *this* going on?" or, "All that enlightenment jazz sounded great when things were smooth, but now? Ha!" But when the going gets tough, the tough get sitting. This is precisely the time to apply our deepest skills and widest perspective—not to evade or deny the hard situation, but, on the contrary, to see it with clear eyes, unclouded by our old assumptions and habits. For me, that challenge in its sharpest form was the illness and death of my first wife, the mother of my children. If I may say so, that gave me the authority to testify that the stuff works.

∽

What about the challenges of the wider world—global warming, rising inequality, offensively stupid politics? Some people argue that meditation and spiritual development are cop-outs, pacifiers, feel-good methods for shirking real-world problems. But it's not either/or. As always, you do what you see your way clear to do, whatever action or activism may call you. Meditation is not the opium of the people.

This issue—the inner vs. the outer approach to saving the world—was addressed over two thousand years ago in the Bhagavad Gita. The answer it gives is that you do both, and that the two are not in conflict but complementary. The Gita tells the story of how Lord Krishna, an embodiment of highest truth, instructs the warrior Arjuna in the middle of a great battlefield just before the fighting breaks out. He teaches him first to dive within to the silent core of being, then to come out to fight his battle with greater dynamism than ever. Arjuna is a great archer, and this two-step process is like first pulling the arrow back on the bow, then letting it fly.

And now, as with the pursuit of personal happiness, you're coming from a place of fullness rather than lack. Your campaign for a saner, kinder, more enlightened world becomes more credible and effective as you become a saner, kinder, more enlightened person. After all, the world is made up of persons, just like you, and although (as Sting put it) we go crazy in congregations, we get better one by one.

The Bhagavad Gita also teaches the importance of pursuing your own *dharma*—your life-path, the way of participating and contributing in the world that is most natural and appropriate to you. You need to choose (or, rather, recognize) your own battlefield and your own weapons. I don't buy the idea that anyone who's not a social or political activist is morally delinquent. Some people contribute far more to humanity by being a great musician or teacher than a lousy activist. "Better is death in one's own dharma than life in the dharma of another," teaches the Gita—a more elevated way of saying, "Do your own thing."

My friend Ian spent five years training to be a dentist before he realized that as a dentist he'd be miserable; he'd fix some teeth but would be radiating misery into the world. He eventually found his calling as a financial advisor, helping people manage their money wisely so that they and their families can achieve their goals. He loves doing it, and his clients love him. My friend Maurice owns a successful business but also pursues his real passion as a master woodworker. Me, I get head pressure just looking at a tax form, and I can't use a hammer without damaging something, usually myself. If there weren't dharmas consisting of writing and talking, I'd be in the gutter.

> ADRIAN: Why do you wanna fight?
> ROCKY: Because I can't sing or dance.
> —*Rocky*

There's one more vital teaching of the Bhagavad Gita that unfolds for us as we live the meditative life: *action without attachment to its outcome*. This point is frequently misunderstood. It doesn't mean apathy, indifference, or resignation. Nor is it a noble sacrifice. Krishna's words in the Gita are, "You have jurisdiction over your actions only, never their fruits." That's a statement of pure scientific fact. We do what we do, which is hopefully in accord with our dharma, and we do it as skillfully, sensitively, and conscientiously as we can. Then whatever happens happens. It's not even a matter of letting the chips fall where they may, but rather recognizing that they're gonna, no matter what we do or don't "let." Again, Rocky to Adrian:

> It really don't matter if I lose this fight. It really don't matter if this guy opens my head either. 'Cause all I wanna do is go the distance. Nobody's ever gone the distance with Creed, and if I can go that distance, you see, and that bell rings and I'm still standin', I'm gonna know for the first time in my life, see, that I weren't just another bum from the neighborhood.

All you have to do is go the distance with life, and you do it by staying naturally focused on throwing *this* punch in *this* moment, just as we've focused on drawing a single breath. If you can do this, it's utterly liberating. You become so grounded in impeccably performing *this* action that you let go of everything else, including the whole imaginary realm of feared or desired results, which you never had in your grasp to begin with.

Then action without attachment becomes a form of meditation as much as anything you do with your eyes closed. In the Gita, it's called *karma yoga*, "union [with beingness] through action." If you've ever, say, cared for a terminally ill loved one, you've probably practiced karma yoga, plunging so completely into the work at hand that everything else falls away—even knowing that ultimately she'll die anyway. There's nothing to do about it but fling all your hopes and fears into the fire of right-now, on-the-ball service. And in the middle of that service, you may have noticed a strange, quiet, deep elation. This is the taste of the liberation, the incredible lightness that comes from dropping the weight of hopes and fears, and it doesn't make us one ounce less conscientious. It's the same luminous spaciousness that we've been talking about all along. Eventually, you can do everything from there.

All kinds of ideals and truths that once seemed abstract may start becoming lived life. Some people who already feel connected to a religion find that the dry bones of belief and ritual start getting fleshed out with something juicier. Catholics may find that the Holy Spirit is no longer just the most mysterious, abstract member of the Trinity, but an immediate, intimate fact of life, the One Taste that suffuses all things. Muslims may find that *Tawhid*, the ineffable oneness that is the prime attribute of Allah, becomes less a theological doctrine and more the warp and woof of daily living. Jews who have attended Passover Seders their whole lives—celebrating their deliverance out of bondage, and even reciting verses stating that this deliverance is not only for their ancestors but for themselves—may start to truly experience that deliverance. Mizraim, the biblical name for Egypt, literally means "the narrow, constricted places," as well as "worry, distress." *That's* what we're delivered from: it's not just some tribal history about vacating one piece of real estate and finding another.

As the expansive nature of being grows more intimately familiar to you, here's a simple way you can bring it into your religion: Just before you sing the *Shema* or drink the communion wine or light the incense to Ma Lakshmi, take a moment—perhaps the space of one breath, in and then out—to let your attention settle and spread into that spaciousness. Then consciously bring the spaciousness into the ritual. Later on, you won't even have to take a moment to "bring" it. You'll realize that it was always there *in* the ritual . . . and everywhere else.

There are people (and they may belong to any religion, or none) who since childhood have sensed this spaciousness as a *presence*—an indefinable something. They may have caught only fleeting glimpses of it, perhaps when alone in the woods or beside the sea, but somehow they know it's always there. They can't explain it to anyone else, and probably don't try; it's too delicate a secret to share. It doesn't do anything and it doesn't say anything, but in some mysterious yet self-evident way it is the reassurance that, no matter what happens, everything is all right. For such people, the great discovery now is that those fleeting glimpses are starting to open into an entire, permanent dimension of life . . . and that there is no distance between that dimension and themselves.

All religions have their codes of conduct, their Commandments or Precepts. If you're even a semigrown-up, you know the drill: pay your bills, signal your turns, don't leave your dishes in the sink, don't diddle your neighbor's wife or husband. But following the code can be hard, which is why there's confession and purification. It's also why there's the law of karma, which is nothing mystical, just pure physics: action and reaction. One way or another, you don't get away with anything. As the saying goes, "He who shits in the road will meet flies upon his return." On a deeper level, though, which is now starting to become *our* level, the rules are not so much *pre*scriptive as *de*scriptive—descriptions of the spontaneous behavior of an awakened person. We depend less on the rules to tell us what's right, or on karma to drop anvils on our heads when we get it wrong. More and more, the path of right choices just opens at our feet. We don't even feel we're choosing. It's obvious.

The same goes for all that homely folk wisdom and pop psychology, the cheesy sentiments you see on people's Facebook posts or refrigerator magnets—about loving everyone, and finding your happiness within, and never losing hope, and not letting other people define you, and daring to dream, and dreaming the impossible dream, and letting your dreams take wing. As it turns out, they're not cheesy of themselves, but were only rendered cheeselike by the lack of a natural, authentic way to live them. Now that's changing for you.

One good, concise summary of enlightened behavior comes, as it happens, from the actor Ryan Gosling:

> If you're ever in a situation . . . and you don't know what to do, just be Bugs. Never be Daffy.

Again great advice, but how do you *do* it? Well, now we're doing it. As the scrambled brain waves of our chaotic Daffy Duck–ness gradually evaporate, it gets easier to act with the cool, nonchalant skill of a Bugs Bunny: to see and deal with things as they *are*, rather than filtered through a flurry of mental static. Our signal-to-noise ratio keeps improving.

That quieter mental background also gives you the ability to truly *listen* to others—without your mind churning away the whole time, trying to crank out clever replies. You listen from the silence, from zero, which is true listening. You become a clear lake to reflect the other person's situation back to them, not chopped up by a bunch of your own ripples. Sometimes you don't need to reply at all. When people tell you their troubles, what they really want is healing, and pouring the chaos of their troubles into an ear that's a funnel into bottomless silence is often the most healing thing that can happen. When it's time to speak, you'll know it, and your words will be steeped in that silence, imbued with its power. Otherwise, like King Lear's daughter Cordelia, just "Love, and be silent."

The rate and the particular course of this transformation is different for everyone. Some of it can take years. But flashes of any of it can visit anyone at any time, and often do. If you leave a little room for these flashes and pay some attention to them, so you see that they're part of a larger, ongoing process, you'll be inspired to stay the path. It all comes back to regular practice, even for a minute a day.

And the practice itself changes. Sometimes it may seem very settled and blissful, sometimes utterly boring. That doesn't matter. In these early days of practice, the luscious One Taste plays hide-and-seek with us (there it is—no—yes—no), but over time it gets clearer and sticks around longer. And over time, the meditation itself becomes less to do. Actually, you start to see that there's *nothing* to do, and there was *always* nothing to do. If some effort was there at the beginning, that's OK. Useless, but OK. If you start making effort to remove the effort, things get tail-chasingly complicated. But if you keep coming back to the main principle of natural meditation—leaving things as they are—then effort melts away on its own. You'll make as much effort as you need to make till you see that you never needed to make any at all.

The *results* of meditation also have their ups and downs. Sometimes you'll feel, "Zip-a-dee-doo-dah, I'm enlightened now!" and sometimes you'll feel, "Womp womp, nothing's happened, nothing's *ever* happened." Everyone goes through that. The sages are just the ones that kept going. They understand that this journey is like a train ride. Sometimes you see the scenery whipping past and know you're burning up the miles; sometimes you go into a long tunnel and don't see anything. But when you come out the other end, you'll be amazed at how much distance you've covered.

My old teacher Maharishi loved to cite the traditional Indian method of dying cloth. First you take a piece of white cloth and dip it into a vat of yellow dye. (Maharishi *always* used the color yellow for this analogy. I still can't use any other color.) When you take it out of the vat it's a nice, bright yellow, but it's not yet permanent. So you lay it on a flat rock in the bright sun, which bleaches out most of the color, but a little of it remains colorfast. Then you dip it again, and fade it again, and keep alternating till the cloth is a permanent, bright yellow. In the same way, in meditation we dip our attention into the vat of boundless, delicious being. We come out, and to some degree boundlessness stays with us. Then the sunlight of daily life bleaches most of it out. But that's fine—that's part of the process. A little bit has become permanent. As long as we keep dipping and fading, we're on our way. And the fading is just as important as the dipping.

All this enlightenment talk may seem a little heady. Maybe it's enough to say that things get easier. Our life, which sometimes seemed so complicated and heavy, becomes simpler, lighter, less dense. You see other people still living in complication, and it's clear—sometimes embarrassingly clear—that they're getting in their own way, tripping over the needless complexity generated by their own noisy minds. They're Daffy. And that used to be you.

There are things to be done, but you just do them and move on.

The plot thins.

19. Meditating on Sky

In 2001, I went on a pilgrimage to Tibet. There were about fifteen of us, mostly Westerners, and we took off from Kathmandu on a small China Airlines jet. Below us the Himalayas were invisible, shrouded in clouds . . . but suddenly everyone was running to the windows on the left side. Poking up through the cloud cover, brilliant in the sunlight, was the peak of Mount Everest—Chomolungma, the Holy Mother. Meanwhile, on the ceiling-mounted TV sets that ran the length of the aisle, a *Tom and Jerry* cartoon played. (Sublime + ridiculous = life.)

Then we landed in Lhasa, the capital city, and walked down the ramp onto the tarmac. It was my first time at that altitude—over eleven thousand feet—and I immediately noticed the sort of light-headed, pixilated, Champagne feeling that I had heard about. I also felt as if I were seeing the first truly clear sky of my life. It was perfectly cloudless, but, more than that, the atmosphere at that altitude was so thin, and the desert air so dry, that it was as if all the clearest skies I had ever seen before had been covered with a gauzy film, and now it had been scraped off.

Over the next few weeks we saw more of that sky, as we trekked to temples and villages above sixteen thousand feet and looked out over panoramic vistas that we had difficulty believing were on planet Earth: sheer cliffs, deep ravines, rings of lunar mountains looming over vast plains and turquoise lakes . . . and above it all that impossibly clear, gaping sky, like a dome that has been opened wide to the vastness of the universe.

It was on that trip that I came to understand why a Tibetan specialty for centuries has been *namkhai-nyaljor*: skygazing meditation.

~

Find a place to sit where you have an unobstructed view of the open sky, or at least enough of it to fill most of your visual field.

Since you'll be looking up, this method lends itself well to using a deck chair or a hammock, or spreading a blanket on the ground. It's also fine to do this indoors, looking out a window. One lama, a refugee from Tibet, had a special window installed in his home, high up near the ceiling, with a reclining chair placed strategically so he could practice skygazing in the comfort of his living room.

If you're sitting rather than lying down, the classical posture for this technique is one of wide openness, with your knees splayed apart and your hands resting loosely on them, palms down.

Keep your eyes open . . . not staring, not trying not to blink, but gazing in a natural, relaxed way into the open sky.

Take a deep breath and then intone *ahhhhhhh*, the mantra of openness.

As you do so, have the feeling of the mantra going out into the sky in all directions, 360 degrees.

Do this three times.

Now let your mouth remain slightly open, as if you're still saying *ahhhhhhh*. This has the added advantage of making you feel a little stupid, as if you're saying *duh*. We've given up trying to figure things out. (When a plane or a bird crosses your field of vision, the mind may try to get back into the act, trying to latch on to *something* in that vast openness: "Bird! Probably flying south for the winter . . . or is that north?" Of course you just ignore those thoughts.)

Let the breath be natural. Don't be concerned whether it's flowing through the nose or mouth or both.

Let the jaw be soft, relaxed . . .

and let that be a cue for all the muscles of the face to be soft and relaxed . . .

and all the muscles of the body to be soft and relaxed.

At any time during the session, if you feel you're getting antsy, or you've lost the sense of resting in openness, or you just need to refresh things, you can close your eyes for a bit, then press the reset button by opening them and starting again with the three *ahhhhhhh*'s.

Eyes open . . .

ears open . . .

gaze open . . .

mouth open . . .

body open . . .

all the pores of your skin open . . .

breathing open . . .

mind open . . .

everything naturally open.

Not trying or straining for more openness, but everything just left open, like a window that someone forgot to close . . .

the entire body and mind like a house with all its windows and doors left open . . .

and the roof and walls left open . . .

so that all the breezes can blow through.

Notice that this openness is like the openness of the sky.

Continue to rest your open gaze in the openness of the sky.

In its own time, allow the openness of your gaze, your body, your breath, and your awareness to merge with the openness of the sky . . .

so that all that remains is undifferentiated openness.

Continue to rest in that.

Continue to rest *as* that.

As you'll see after one or two sessions, this is a beautiful method. Like the meditation on self and other, it helps dissolve the sense of being a separate, isolated, limited entity. And it shows us that we can settle just as profoundly with the eyes open as closed. (You can even sneak this in at the office: just gaze past the edges of your computer monitor and you'll look like you're working.)

That's an important discovery. It goes a long way toward breaking down the distinction—the artificial distinction, it turns out—between "meditation" and "life." If we don't need to close our eyes to be in the expansive space of meditation, what else don't we need to do? Sit down? Stay in one place? Be silent? Be alone? All this bears exploration.

One more discovery you may make is that the sky is everywhere. Gazing into the unobstructed sky is, in a sense, training wheels for gazing into the living room, classroom, library, subway car, office cubicle, jail cell, or wherever else you may find yourself. It's all sky. We might look up at the stars and planets and marvel at the vast space in which they float, but we're always floating in it as much as they are. People on Mars or in the Andromeda galaxy might be looking up at *us* and marveling.

Don't worry that there's a wall full of family photos or a shelf full of books smack in the middle of your view. Treat everything in your visual field exactly as you treat sounds or thoughts in meditation. It's just stuff that's there: landscape, soundscape, thoughtscape—all just ripples on the sea of awareness. If some of the visual material (say the family photos) stimulates thought material ("Whatever happened to Uncle Al?"), recognize that those thoughts also are just ripples on the sea. Don't try to push any of it away, but don't engage with it either.

In fact, after you've practiced with nice, open sky for a while, it's *good* to confront a cluttered visual field. Vision is the dominant sense for humans, which is why we don't have big snouts like dogs. It plays the major role in leading our attention and defining our reality. What we're really discovering by gazing into the sky is the vast, skylike nature of our own awareness. Just as the sky can never be diminished by the appearance of clouds, our skylike awareness can never be diminished by any kind of so-called clutter, whether in our visual field, our mind, or anywhere else.

> *Enlightenment is nothing other than the spontaneous experience of all possible structures as equivalent to open space.*
>
> —PRAJNAPARAMITA SUTRA

By realizing the spacious, skylike nature of our awareness, we come to realize the spacious, skylike nature of our lives.

20. Tips and Flashes

I've sometimes had the experience of rereading a wise book for the third or fifth time, when—BLAM! There's some stunning, mind-blowing, skull-shattering, sky-opening statement that in one moment vaporizes all my confusion, or some exquisitely subtle instruction that instantly makes everything fall into place. And I say, "Wait a minute! How did *that* get in there? I swear it wasn't there before!"

I've had a similar thing happen when listening to recordings of my teachers, even in cases where I was the one asking the question. There seems to be a mysterious phenomenon that can keep us from hearing or seeing things till we're at a place where they'll be meaningful to us. I think this is why Jesus sometimes punctuates his teachings with the refrain, "Those who have ears to hear, let them hear."

You may find this to be true of this book. After you get to the end, I suggest that you keep it around, pick it up from time to time, and crack it open to a page at random. You may be surprised at how often this brings you to just the reminder you need, and how often you'll be convinced you're seeing it for the first time.

In keeping with this sort of serendipitous, Magic 8 Ball process, this chapter is a grab bag of snippets and stories, in no particular order. Some of them may not speak to you now, but they will later. Some of them may stop you in your tracks. You might recall the saying we cited earlier, that we need strong hands and feet for climbing (effective meditative practice) and good eyes for seeing (clear insight). The snippets here apply to both: they include practical tips as well as flashes of insight, from me and from others.

❧

Don't think. Look.

❧

Keep cracking it open. Take little moments throughout the day to close your eyes, settle into simple silence, and just be: before a meal, in the shower, at the red light, in the airport, in the doctor's office, while standing at the kitchen counter waiting for your toast to pop. Keep dipping in and out till you see there's no in or out. In this way, you integrate being and doing. More and more, you'll find that there's no real difference between eyes open and eyes closed, between red light and green light. You do what you have to do (stop on the red, go on the green), but the being-aware-ness remains the same: pure, unassailable, unavoidable, inexplicable, simple beyond simple.

❧

Time is what eternity looks like when filtered through the mind.

—RUPERT SPIRA

～

Somewhere there's a bar where Jesus, Moses, Buddha, Al-Hallaj, Lao-Tzu, Shankara, the Ba'al Shem Tov, and all the rest of their cosmic buddies take turns telling stories, buying the next round, and laughing. Outside on the sidewalk, their followers argue.

～

A legend:

When God decided to create human beings, the angels were jealous, for angels had not been created in the divine image. The angels plotted to hide the divine image from human beings. One suggested burying it in the depths of the sea; another in the crag of a jagged mountain peak. But the most clever of the angels suggested, "No. Let us hide the divine image within each person. It's the last place they'll ever look."

—MIDRASH

～

Every time you take a flight, at the end of the safety spiel the friendly voice invites you to "sit back." That's a lesson in relaxation from a corporation that has billions of dollars invested in keeping planefuls of people as relaxed and happy as possible.

When in doubt, sit a little farther back. Whether meditating or doing anything else, it's good to check this occasionally. When we think we're vertical, we're often subtly leaning forward, especially now that so many of us spend our days leaning into computer screens. If you feel tension in your neck, you're probably leaning slightly forward and then rocking your head back to compensate. This puts strain on your neck and restricts your breathing. Sit back and let your neck rise like a cobra.

~

Life is Pac-Man.

You go round and round the maze, gobbling as many power pellets (achievement, approval, money, success) as you can, while evading the lethal ghosts (failure, humiliation, disease, death) for as long as you can. In the traditional teachings, this kind of endlessly cyclic, going-nowhere existence is called *samsara*.

The opposite of samsara is nirvana. By dipping a toe or a foot or a couple of legs into nirvana every day in your meditative practice, you gradually drain the urgency out of the game. It still goes on for some time, at least outwardly, and you play with sharper skill than ever, but you're just not gripped by it the way you used to be. More and more, the game goes on without you.

~

It is not civilized to want other people to believe what you believe because the essence of being civilized is to possess yourself as you are, and if you

possess yourself as you are you of course cannot possess anyone else, it is
not your business.

—GERTRUDE STEIN

~

Life grows spacious. Not spacey, not mushy, but crisp, clear, precise: high-resolution perception of all the details and of the open, detailless space in which they float.

~

The Buddha was bald, shaven headed like all the monks in his group. The tightly curled hair you see on his pictures and statues is due to the influence of Greek sculpture. He discouraged graven images, and after his death many years had to pass before Buddhist artists ventured to ignore his wishes and make images of him. We can assume that the Buddhas we see today are as much a fantasy as the fair-skinned, straight-haired Euro-Jesus of Western religious art.

None of this matters. In spirituality as in love, we use forms that attract and delight us as doorways into the Formless. Just don't get stuck on the form.

~

"*Mom-m-m,* I'm bored!" You first whined that in childhood, and have probably said or thought it hundreds of times since. But next time it happens, ask yourself, "How do I *know* I'm bored?" Really look. What are the signals that tell you that? Usually we move so quickly from "I'm bored" to searching for distracting stimuli that we have no idea how we know. So look.

Maybe you'll find that it's just a concept, a habitual thought that says whenever the amount of action on our mental screen dips below a certain level, that's called boredom and it's unpleasant. Or maybe you'll find that, as with fear and anger, there are some subtle physical sensations involved, and they're just . . . sensations.

Either it's just a thought or it's just a sensation. Either way, it's not you. You are the luminous, empty awareness that's aware of it. Instead of automatically (slavishly) searching for stimuli, rest as that awareness . . . and suddenly the whole thing melts out from under you, and you're free again.

~

I used to have a small bell with a beautiful, pure, chimelike sound. Whenever I led a group meditation I would start it by slowly striking the bell three times. Afterward, people would tell me, "Oh, I love that bell. When I hear it I go right into the zone. I've gotta get me a bell like that." So I stopped using it.

~

Notice how your skill of opening your pores and soaking in the hot tub of meditation carries over into other situations. You know how to let go, be fully present, and give yourself over to fully soaking: soaking in the green of the park or woods, soaking in art or music, soaking in laughter.

~

The Mundaka Upanishad, one of India's great wisdom texts, uses a vivid image to portray the nature of enlightenment:

> Two birds of beautiful plumage, inseparably united in friendship, reside on the self-same tree. One of them eats the sweet fruit of the tree, the other witnesses without eating.

The limited doing-self stays busily engaged in the world, consuming all that it offers. The limitless being-Self does nothing, consumes nothing, needs nothing, silently witnesses everything. But there's no conflict between them, just two aspects of the same life. They're inseparable friends on the self-same tree.

~

You have turned my mourning into dancing.

—PSALM 30:11

~

One other thing the friendly voice says in that in-flight safety spiel: be sure your own oxygen mask is secured before attempting to help others.

∾

I once stayed at a hotel with an infinity pool. You start walking in right from the deck, where the water is zero inches deep. From there, it slopes incrementally till your feet no longer reach the bottom.

Sooner or later we notice that everything's an Infinity Pool. Each person or object, when you first encounter it, starts at the deck level of ordinary life, but eventually opens to infinite depth. Moon is Infinity Moon, garden is Infinity Garden, saxophone solo is Infinity Saxophone Solo, lover is Infinity Lover.

∾

Mike, a guitar player I sometimes jam with, told me about a woman he knew who was in the hospital. A mutual friend went to visit her there, then texted Mike that the woman had died of pneumonia . . . but her iPhone's autocorrect changed it to "phenomena." Well, eventually we all die of phenomena, don't we?

Actually, these *bodies* are phenomena, and *they* die of phenomena. We are the witness of phenomena.

∾

Heaven is this moment. Hell is the burning desire for this moment to be different. It's that simple.

—JEFF FOSTER

∾

Without opening—somehow—to this inner richness, life is just . . . *meh*. It's like the Jerry Seinfeld joke about Pop-Tarts: they're never stale because they were never fresh.

∾

"*I am a dream that can wake you up.*"
—SRI NISARGADATTA MAHARAJ

∾

When people say, "I'm working on myself," are they the one that's being worked on or the one that's doing the work? Or neither?
Discuss.

∾

These bodies are here for a while, part of something bigger, like leaves on a tree. Eventually they grow dry and fragile, till just the breeze or gale required comes along and flies them to the ground, just in time. There's nothing tragic in this. In fact, it's completely natural and beautiful . . . if you know you're the tree. If you think you're a leaf, and if medical science and your health insurance keep offering you new, improved varieties of Crazy Glue, you may keep clinging to your twig way past your

time, eking out a few more arduous weeks or months to distract yourself from what you are, which is eternity.

~

Hey, this is important.

This applies to any meditation we're doing, and it's at least as important as which specific technique we do. By all means do the technique
and see where it leads you, but . . .

> **Don't look for another, different experience outside of**
> **whatever's being experienced right now, in this moment.**

The present moment is reality. It's our only reality. It's always already
here. It's always all we have. And it's always too late to change it.

When you try to change the experience of the present moment,
you're trying to replace reality with a concept. That doesn't work. Never-
theless, everyone tries. Everyone who has ever meditated has probably
tried, the Buddha included. If we're lucky or smart or have skillful guides
(and listen to them), sooner or later we realize that trying doesn't work
and we give up. We can always choose sooner.

When you do realize that you've been searching for some experience
other than what's presenting itself in the present, simply recognize that
that searching is the result of buying into the thought, "Something else
should be happening—where is it?" As with any other thought, just ignore it.

Whatever's there, just rest aware.

Leave it as it is. You can't do anything about it, and you don't *have* to
do anything about it. It all happens by itself. You try to swim here, you

try to swim there, till you give up and let the current carry you. Finally, you surrender.

～

The boardwalk ... dusk ... dogs on leashes, tongues hanging out, racing along with their owners on bikes or skateboards . . . freedom . . . joy. That's what your life is becoming. Bob Dylan has a droll song about this, "If Dogs Run Free," where he asks, "Then why not we?"

～

You may find yourself tuning into this freer, more joyful, more flowing style on the dance floor, as well as on the dance floor of life. There's less inhibition, less trying to imitate other people's moves, less concern about whether they think your moves are cool. Whether it's the music of music or the music of life, just feel it with your body and let it move you. Not worrying about whether your moves are cool makes them cool. Not worrying about how they look makes them graceful and beautiful.

～

Teaching is the art of seeing the wisdom in the student's confusion and showing it to him.

～

"No one is anything."

—JAMES JOYCE, *Ulysses*

~

On Facebook, I've listed my employer as Self. Now my profile says, "Works at Self," which is not really true—it's not something you work at. Facebook also keeps asking me, "When did you start at Self?" Well, that's hard to say.

~

My wife is a documentary film editor who occasionally works on "reality" shows. The quotation marks are there for a reason. People often think an editor receives something called a film, which she then trims and tweaks a bit—cuts out the bloopers. But in fact she usually receives a mountain of footage, out of which she chooses "selects," with which she then builds a story: a structure that arcs from beginning to middle to end, populated by characters, whom she can make heroic or villainous by the art of selection and assemblage.

The mind is *our* editor, culling out a small portion of the raw footage of our actual experience, assembling it into a story that pulls the desired emotional strings and expresses the desired themes, interpreting people as characters we like or dislike, and with all these elements building a "reality." And that's OK, as long as we know it's just a show.

∽

The more you look at the same exact thing, the more the meaning goes away, and the better and emptier you feel.

—ANDY WARHOL

∽

Closing your eyes for a few moments whenever you sit down to eat is especially good. This injects an extra dose of silence into your routine a couple of times a day, allowing all your busyness to settle down, making mealtime a little island of peace. That's good for your digestion, good for your relationship, good for interrupting any headlong rush into unconscious overeating—just good. Sometimes if you've been cooking, hustling around the kitchen to get the food on the table, you may find that you're still caught up in that speedy, hustling vibe when you sit down. If so, you can take a deep breath, then release it slowly and consciously. Then sit back and enjoy your meal like royalty.

∽

To live a life without having any fundamental expectations of anybody: this is a great freedom. You find that you are almost unshockable, because something inside has switched off the button of how things should be.

—MOOJI

～

In their dreams, people often experience themselves as a faceless awareness, an unembodied presence witnessing the action. What if that's what you are all the time? See if it's so.

～

Naren Schreiner, a wonderful singing teacher I've studied with who is deeply steeped in the musical and spiritual traditions of India, told our class this story:

One day Emperor Akbar praised his court musician, Miyan Tansen. "Surely," he said, "you must be the finest singer in the world."

"Thank you, your highness," Tansen replied, "but I cannot accept that praise. My teacher is far superior."

"Well," said the emperor, "I doubt that that's true, but let us have him brought to the court and hear him."

"I'm afraid that's not possible. My guru-ji lives a simple life in a small hut in the forest, and he won't leave it for anyone—not even the emperor."

"Then I will go to him. Bring me to the place."

"I can do that, but I cannot promise that he'll sing."

Tansen led the emperor through the thick forest until they came to the hut. There Hari Das, the old singing master, received the two visitors politely but took no special notice of the emperor. When they both en-treated him to sing, he acted as if he didn't hear them. Then Tansen had an idea. He began to sing a hymn, with a few deliberate imperfections in his rendition. Although the flaws were very subtle, he knew his guru would notice them and, being a true teacher, could not resist giving his student proper guidance. The old master sang the hymn correctly—and with a sky-melting power in his voice that the emperor had never thought possible.

As they walked back toward the palace, the emperor said, "Well, you were right. Your guru is the greatest singer. But I'm sure that someday you'll ascend to his level."

"No, your highness," Tansen replied. "That will never happen."

"But why not?"

"Because my guru sings only for God. I sing for you."

The room went silent; we were all deeply moved by this story. But I kept thinking about it, and after class I asked Naren, "What if he sang to the God he saw in the emperor's eyes?"

~

Other people's problems seem so unreal; ours seem so real. See if you can flip these two.

~

Not "Revelation" 'tis that waits,
But our unfurnished eyes.
—EMILY DICKINSON

≈

Pharrell Williams nailed it in that "Happy" song. Enlightenment is the happiness that makes you *feel like a room without a roof.* On the mundane, horizontal plane of life, you're a room: a confined, walled-off space. On the vertical plane, no roof: open space, boundless sky, limitless being.

In our age, evidently, divine truth can come in the form of a bubbly pop tune. People all over the world respond to it, dance to it, post their videos online, and on some level absorb its message. They *clap along* because intuitively they *feel like happiness is the truth*—that ananda, life's essential deliciousness, is ultimate reality.

And since that *sunshine she's here,* we can all *take a break.* That's what you've been learning to do in this book.

≈

I love you. It's nothing personal.

≈

When you're not busy fighting ghosts, your love can just flow—your joy knows no bounds.

—MOOJI

≈

Raving lunatics, the ones you'll see on the streets of many cities, are messengers. They're like funhouse mirrors showing you your own mind, just stretched and distorted a bit. If you listen to a few moments of their ravings, you'll notice that their lunacy is due to an overdose of thoughts and personal self—or, rather, of *believing* in their thoughts and personal self. Just like us, only more so. To be stuck in that is hell. You can inwardly thank these beings for the lesson, and, so that their suffering is not in vain, apply it diligently.

~

Instead of clearing his own heart, the zealot tries to clear the world.
—JOSEPH CAMPBELL

~

Just drop your concepts and be.

That simple.

"But—"

That "But," and whatever was going to follow it, is also a concept: drop it. For one minute, ten seconds, one second if that's what you can manage, just drop your concepts and be. Rest assured, they'll be waiting for you when you're done, right where you dropped them. You can pick them up again any time you want—*if* you want.

Just drop your concepts and be—your concepts that life is lovely or sucky, that we're shaped by this or that past and we face this or that future, that you're this or that kind of person. You don't have to go painstakingly through a list like this. Painstakingly and one by one is how you accumulated your concepts, but you can drop them all, en masse, in one moment.

Just drop your concepts and be. "But how do I *do* that?" someone once asked Mooji. He smiled and said, "How do you drop a hot potato?" Then, as if pronouncing the title of a cheesy self-help book, he said, "*Ten Easy Ways to Drop a Hot Potato.*"

Just drop your concepts and be. If you have ears to hear those six words, and can put them into practice, dropping the hot potato of your concepts again and again till you no longer find it back in your hand, you can drop all other meditative practices as well.

Just drop your concepts and be. Perhaps most people *won't* hear and do this. Perhaps it's too direct, too frontal an assault on all the conceptual baggage they've acquired and packed so carefully for all these years and have worked so hard to lug. But some will hear it and do it.

~

Jesus said, "Be passersby."

—THE GOSPEL OF THOMAS

~

A traditional analogy for thoughts, awareness, and meditation:

Say you have a jar of muddy water, and you take on the job of clearing the mud out of it. You try shaking it, stirring it, scooping the mud out with a spoon. Eventually, when one strategy after another has failed, you give up and set the jar down on the table. But when you come back later you see that, by just letting it sit and leaving it as it is, you have allowed the mud to settle, in its own time and in its own way, all by itself. The sparkling clarity of the water—which was there all the time, its essential nature—spontaneously shines forth.

～

Love is not a feeling; it's lack of an other, of otherness. Happiness is not a pleasant mental state, but absence of a sense of lack.

—RUPERT SPIRA

～

Some people have a habitual "busy tune" that runs through their heads as they go from task to task. (Mine is an instrumental medley of "Bandstand Boogie" and "Jumpin' with Symphony Sid," with an occasional snatch of "Surfin' U.S.A." Go figure.) No problem. But when you recognize that the busy tune is there—that it's not silence—you can penetrate it and hear the silence beneath it.

～

Another traditional analogy:

When an ordinary person registers an emotion or impression, it's like carving a line in rock. When an enlightened person registers an emotion or impression, it's like drawing a line in water: it's still drawn, but it closes immediately. Some say that, in very advanced stages of enlightenment, it's like drawing a line in air.

~

People often think enlightenment means you're left without emotions, but that's backward. The emotions are left without a personal "you."

~

Perhaps all your life you think of happiness as something dangling in front of you, which you'll catch up with sooner or later. Then, when you start to meditate, it's natural that, for a while, you keep reaching forward, even subtly, trying to catch up to it in your meditation. Eventually it becomes clear that happiness was, all along, the one who was reaching. You thought it was some amazing roadside attraction you were going to drive to, and it turns out that it's more like backing into the garage. Or discovering that you never left the garage. Or that you *are* the garage.

~

Imagine that you've written a book titled *My Story*—your meticulously compiled, moment-by-moment, blow-by-blow, then-she-said-then-I-said autobiography. Really, close your eyes and imagine that book. And now imagine that you throw it into the fire.

How's that feel? Maybe kind of scary . . . but also kind of a relief?

Now imagine that you've written the companion volume: *My*

Thoughts. Everything you've so carefully worked out over a lifetime about philosophy, religion, politics, who's who, what's what, what's hot, what's not . . . and now throw *it* into the fire.

Refreshing?

You're welcome.

~

If you're suffering, find the sufferer.

~

I was once on a retreat led by Tsoknyi Rinpoche, a wonderful, wise, and often very funny lama from Nepal. At one teaching session I told him that in my "official" sitting meditations my mind often felt fidgety and busy, but during informal walking meditation I usually felt deep inner silence. And so, I asked, should I sit more or walk more?

Without missing a beat he answered, "Both!"

~

We create many stories about other people. Sometimes we might form a negative impression of someone ("That flight attendant is such a bitch!"; "That guy always stiffs me on my tip!"), and then we're quietly disappointed when they fail to live up to the role in which we've cast them, depriving us of another chance to be indignant. This is just the mind's mischief. If you simply recognize it as mischief, it's harmless. Have another good laugh at yourself.

～

I saw that love freed me into the ocean and righteousness didn't, and that
I'd rather be free than right.

—RAM DASS

～

You know that voice you've been hearing in your head, chattering away your whole life? Who is it talking to? And who's the one that's talking? And which one is you?

Actually, neither is you. You're the silent awareness-space within which both the chattering and the listening take place. They're like two puppets, and you're the empty puppet stage on which they play.

Look and see if it's so.

～

The standard worldview—that we are objects called bodies, which scramble to extract scarce doses of happiness from other objects for a limited time, and then die—is naturally terrifying. For most of the people you know, that terror hovers in the background of every moment. Their behavior can't help but be distorted by it, and we can scarcely help feeling compassion for them. It is (in a traditional metaphor) like living with a tiger in your house.

But when you catch a glimpse of the actuality—that we're not doomed, time-bound objects but timeless awareness, that we don't need to seek happiness because we *are* happiness—then you see that it's a paper tiger. Because the old view is an ingrained habit that's reinforced by our culture from every side, most people need several glimpses before they fully let go of that view. But even one glimpse can never be undone. You can never again be completely terrified by a paper tiger.

~

When you hug people, don't get stuck at the level of the body. Hug their presence with your presence, their innocence with your innocence, their beingness with your beingness.

~

Sometimes during sitting, you'll feel frustrated: "I don't know what I'm doing, I have no idea how to meditate." That's great. In fact, that's the best. *No . . . idea*. What are ideas but thoughts? Now that you've stopped listening to your thoughts, you have no choice but to give up. When you run out of things to do, there's nothing left but to be.

This applies to your life off the cushion as well.

I will lead the blind by a road they do not know; by paths they have not known I will guide them. I will turn the darkness before them into light, the rough places into level ground. These are the things I will do, and I will not forsake them.

—ISAIAH 42:16

21. Meditating on I

Please try this:

Hold one hand out in front of you and wiggle your fingers slowly, serenely. You're aware of a tranquil, relaxed activity. Now wiggle them as fast as you can. You're aware of a rushed, frenetic activity.

Two different activities, but what remains the same?

Both are witnessed by the same I, the awareness that's aware of both, untouched by them, silent. The most tranquil activity doesn't enhance the I; the most frantic activity doesn't damage it.

Try wiggling the fingers of both hands at the same time, one hand fast and one slow. This silence, this I, has room for everything.

~

We began this book with the simplest of meditations:

Rest in the I-sense.

Rest in the simple, intuitive sense of being "I," the conscious presence that's always present, witnessing everything, from our childhood birthday parties to our latest sneeze.

If you're madly speeding toward the airport, weaving through traffic, trying to make your flight, and I somehow manage to shout through the window and ask if you exist, your answer will be yes. You don't have to pull over and check, the way you would if I asked your pulse rate. If I ask you the same question when you're lying in your hammock sipping a cool drink, or sitting on the floor and happily sorting through your old blues records, you'll give the same answer without hesitation. If I ask a classroom full of six-year-olds if they exist—or if they're present, or if they're aware—they'll laugh and shout "Yes!" in unison.

Are you aware of these words right now? Sure. That awareness, the "I" that knows "Sure, I'm here, I'm aware," is all we're talking about. It's that simple and obvious.

So, when we do something called meditation, we don't have to mess up that simplicity by looking for anything more. As soon as we turn our attention to the I-sense (and before, actually), here it is, the most intimate, unavoidable fact of life. Just stay with this, abide here, rest your attention here. And by now you've become acclimated to letting your attention settle naturally, without trying to concentrate or control the mind, letting gravity take over in its own time and in its own way, not looking for anything outside this moment.

Having tasted several other varieties of natural meditation, now let's return to this first method, this methodless method. Many people wind up concluding that it's not only the simplest approach but also the most profound—the one to have when you're having only one. So let's look into it more deeply.

∾

What is this "I" like? What, exactly, *is* it?

That question sounds tricky, so let's back into it. Let's see what the I *isn't*, and then see what's left. We can start by taking a sheet of paper, drawing up two columns, and then putting things into one column or the other. At the top of the left-hand column, let's write:

I

Then, just to make sure it's clear what we're talking about, let's add a few synonyms:

(Experiencer, Perceiver, Awareness, Subject)

At the top of the right-hand column, let's write:

STUFF

And then add some synonyms:

(Experiences, Perceived, World, Objects)

Now, please look around the room. In this investigation, we'll need to be like good, sharp detectives. Sherlock Holmes says, "There is nothing like first-hand evidence," so let's pay careful attention to what we actually experience, as opposed to mere speculation. (Holmes also says, "I never guess. It is a shocking habit.") Please take your time, and be sure to confirm each observation for yourself before moving on.

As we look around, we see objects. Or, more precisely, we see visual sensations—shapes and colors—that we associate with objects. Are those visual sensations the experiencer, or stuff that's experienced? Obviously, they're experienced. (There are no trick questions or metaphysical traps here; this is all asked in the most straightforward, commonsensical way possible.) So all visual perceptions, all sights must go in the second column. They're perceived. Simple.

How about sounds? Whether it's the birds singing or our ears ringing, we perceive the sounds, so they also must go in the second column. Likewise for the other senses. We experience taste, smell, and touch. They are *experienced by* this I (which is still undefined). And again, the experiences of the five senses are constantly changing, whether suddenly or gradually, subtly or conspicuously. You might think that the penny that's been sitting on your desk for five years still looks the same,

I (Experiencer, Perceiver, Awareness, Subject)	**STUFF** (Experienced, Perceived, World, Objects)

but in fact it's steadily tarnishing, the light on it keeps shifting, and your eyesight has been slowly deteriorating since childhood.

That takes care of the entire world of the five senses. It's all changing and all experienced. It's other than I.

What about the body? Well, do you experience it? How do I know I *have* a body? I look down and I see it, just as I looked down when I was seven and saw my seven-year-old body. I can hear my speech, breath, and various occasional gastrointestinal sounds. I can taste the minty freshness the toothpaste has left in my mouth, and I can sniff my armpit. I can certainly *feel* the body. Or, rather, I perceive a shifting constellation of feelings that I associate with it: the breeze on my skin, the pressure of my butt on the couch, the slight stiffness in my lower back, the discomfort when I have a headache or indigestion, the relief of a belch or fart. But these are all sense perceptions, so they belong in the second column. The body is experienced. It is not I, the experiencer.

Again, take your time. Make sure you're clear on these matters.

What else do you experience right now? Please observe carefully. Thoughts? OK. I *experience* my thoughts, so put those in the right-hand column. Some people have trouble with this one, by the way; they're so firmly in the habit of being lost in the *content* of their thoughts that they don't realize that thoughts themselves are being experienced. When they start practicing meditation, they observe that thoughts are subtle objects that come and go, with their own subtle textures or flavors that vary from one to another.

So, I can't be my thoughts. That's pretty clear in the case of a garden-variety thought like "Time to feed the cat." For some other thoughts, it may be less obvious. For example, what I call my past actually exists for me only as certain thoughts I have right now in the present, called memories. They're objects of experience—flimsy, unreliable ones, by the way—so I'm not my memories, not my so-called past. No matter how carefully I cultivate and preserve my history, with all its joys and terrors and unique, cherished plot twists, it's not I.

Even flimsier is what I might call my future, which is just a projection: anticipation, hopes, and fears. They're all constructed out of thoughts in the present—clearly a house of straw. I may hold a passionate commitment to some grand imagined destiny (mentally rehearsing my Oscar speech), but I'm not that destiny; I'm the one imagining it.

What about my opinions? My strongest convictions? All thoughts. So if I say I'm a Democrat or a Libertarian or a Muslim or a vegan, I'm not describing what I am. I'm describing thoughts I have ... and memories (more thoughts) about having had them and perhaps acted on them in the past. The more persistently they're experienced—the longer these belief-thoughts hang around—the easier it is to mistake them for the I, to *identify* with them. Hence when my beliefs are threatened I feel that *I'm* threatened, and will defend them at all costs.

Feelings? Same deal. As we've noted before, they're called feelings because they *feel* a certain way. To be startled or elated or angry is to have certain sensations, often not recognized as such, perhaps in the stomach or chest or more generally suffused throughout the body. So feelings belong with the five senses. That's different from the whole who-did-what-to-whom narrative that explains what you're angry *about*. Like all narratives, that's made out of ... thoughts! When someone sits you down to talk about their feelings, the real topic is usually thoughts (memories, hopes, fears, interpretations) connected with situations in which intense feelings have been experienced—or imagined. In any case, feelings, like thoughts, are perceived. I feel the joy or sadness; they don't feel me. I am perceiver, they are perceived. They go in the right-hand column. As with thoughts, when feelings are persistent we tend to identify with them ("I'm an angry young man," "I'm a loving friend," "I'm a bad, guilty daughter," "I'm a happy-go-lucky guy"). Still they're what we feel, not what we are, not the one who feels them.

What does that leave for the left-hand column . . . the perceiver . . . the I?

Not much. In fact, nothing.

That is, no thing, no object—nothing that can be seen, heard, tasted, smelt, felt, or thought. But as we've seen, it's always present and conscious. It's not a *thing* we can be aware *of,* but awareness itself. Since it's

I (Experiencer, Perceiver, Awareness, Subject)	STUFF (Experienced, Perceived, World, Objects)
	sight sound taste smell touch body thoughts feelings

out of the realm of the senses, it can't have any texture, or center, or edge. So it has no perimeter . . . so it's boundless. That doesn't mean it's big, but that the category of size has nothing to do with it. Having no past, present, or future, it can't have a narrative; therefore it can't have flaws, problems, solutions to problems. It can't be entertaining or boring. It can't be young or old, male or female, animal, vegetable, or mineral. Perhaps most shocking of all, *it can't be a person.*

Now we're challenging one of our most firmly held assumptions, so buckle up.

What is a person? Where is it? In your toe, your elbow, your blood, your name? This question was addressed some twenty-two hundred years ago in a famous dialogue between King Milinda, the Greek ruler of India, and the monk Nagasena. When Nagasena asserted that there was no person called Nagasena—no "permanent individuality," as he put it—the king objected. The monk responded by cross-examining him about his chariot, asking whether a chariot is the wheels, or the axle, or the spokes, and so forth.

King Milinda eventually saw that a chariot can't be any of these things, that *chariot* is just a name we agree to call an impermanent, unstable situation in which a bunch of components function together in certain ways. (And nowadays we know that each component is a bunch of smaller components, all the way down to quarks.) If one wheel falls off, is there still a chariot? We'd probably call it a chariot with a missing wheel. But what if two wheels fall off? And then, while the chariot is in the shop, what if the axle is stolen? If it keeps being stripped, at what point does it stop being a chariot? If I turn it on its side and eat my lunch off of it, is it a chariot or a table? Where does the essence of chariotness go, if it ever existed?

Similarly with the person, the "permanent individuality" that we allegedly are. The harder we try to locate it here or there, the faster it breaks down under our gaze. We see that it's just an impermanent, unstable situation in which a bunch of components function together in certain ways, and we all agree to call that situation Nancy or Andrew. It's a vague, sprawling concept, built like a magpie's nest out of scavenged scraps of memories, generalizations, impressions of body images, and so forth. The cells you had when you were seven have long since fallen away, like old chariot wheels. Your whole body is replacement parts.

The words *person* and *personality* both derive from the Greek *persona*, which means "mask." In the ancient Greek drama, the actors wore oversize masks with exaggerated facial features and megaphones built in to amplify their voices. That mask, that artifice, is the person. You are what's *behind* the mask—only it's not even a "what." This insight, that I am not a person or any other thing, but thingless, formless, boundless awareness, may sound very strange—in fact, highly improbable. But by now we've established that I can't be anything else, and as Holmes tells Dr. Watson, "When you have eliminated the impossible, whatever remains, *however improbable*, must be the truth." It's just not possible that I'm anything that's witnessed rather than pure witness.

So, to be a person—even the greatest person in the world, the richest tycoon, the hottest rock star, the most powerful emperor, the most brilliant author, or even the kindest saint—is to reduce yourself to a tottering tower of Legos. Compared with being boundless awareness, that is a life of painful constriction. Fortunately, you can never make yourself a person.

The old Tibetan Dzogchen masters used to wear a small, round mirror of polished brass, called a *melong*, hanging around their necks. They would use it to demonstrate that this formless awareness is like a mirror, which reflects all colors but has no color of its own. It's pure reflectivity. And like the mirror, it's not affected by anything it reflects; it maintains the crystalline purity of its colorlessness, unstained by the sensations, thoughts, and feelings that move frictionlessly across its surface. This awareness which we are has no qualities at all, but reflects all the qualities of ordinary existence. It's the one simple, unitary fact of our life; everything else is complex and plural.

Please try this:

Think of some happy, intensely joyous moment you've had. Close your eyes and let the scene replay itself vividly: the sights, the sounds, the storyline, the feelings. Note that the entire experience appears *within* awareness—where else could it be?—just as the colors appear within the mirror. The awareness remains untouched by it, no matter how intense it is, just as the mirror remains unstained by colors, no matter how bright they are. This doesn't mean that feelings don't or shouldn't arise. It means that feelings are what you feel, while pure awareness is what you *are*.

Now please think of an unhappy, intensely miserable moment you've had. Again, let the scene replay. Again, see that the I-awareness contains it all yet remains untouched.

Now please recall both experiences simultaneously. Note that the I-awareness can even contain opposite poles of experience at once, just like when we simultaneously wiggled the fingers of one hand fast, one hand slow. It is, we could say, "bigger" than all possible experiences—combined—and is still untouched.

Nothing can overshadow what you are.

~

If any of this sounds weird, or bland, or boring, or disappointing, or like an airy-fairy fantasy waiting to be punctured, that's because words are inadequate to convey it—not that it's too complicated for words, but way too simple. Suffice it to say that, over all the centuries that people have been waking to this reality, not one has requested a refund. No one is let down. Everyone says, "This is what I was looking for, even before I knew what to call it. This is what *everyone* is *always* looking for. And it was right here—right *I*—all along." We just keep sleepwalking through life till finally we bump into ourselves.

Trying to discuss this I-awareness conceptually can make it sound mysterious or paradoxical. That's because, just as it's beyond the grasp of the senses, it's also beyond the grasp of the conceptual mind—that is, of thoughts. The thought of "I" is not I; it's just a thought. Thoughts swim within the surface of the awareness-mirror just as the senses do. They will always be too limited to conceive the limitless. We literally can't wrap our minds around it. Trying to get the experience through the words doesn't work; that's backward. But when you experience it, you slap your forehead and say, "Aha! *This* is what all those words meant." It's easier done than said. In fact—as we've been saying all along—it's effortless.

Here's another improbable proposition, Watson:

All beginnings and endings—all births and deaths—belong to the realm of perceivable phenomena. They're in the right-hand column. Therefore you—this formless, nameless, personless perceiver of phenomena—must be birthless and deathless. Sure, that notion seems way, way out there. Yet we all intuitively understand that sages don't worry about dying. And we don't have to look to the time of Jesus or Socrates for examples. When Sri Nisargadatta Maharaj, a great enlightened sage of the mid-twentieth century, contracted throat cancer, he refused all treatment, even painkillers, and continued, unperturbed, to teach in his little Bombay apartment. When a student asked, "What dies with death?" Maharaj replied, "The idea 'I am this body' dies. The witness does not."

Just rest in the I-sense.

By now you know how to sit and settle, naturally and effortlessly, into any vehicle of meditation: breath, sound, heart, sky, or anything else. You know that trying to concentrate or control the mind is like herding kittens—hilariously counterproductive. Now, as we revisit this I meditation, just use that skill of naturalness to settle into the sense of I, the most intimate, taken-for-granted sense there is . . . the one you've had your whole life.

There's only one caveat:

Don't identify the I with anything else.

Maharaj said that this I-sense is like a swinging door. Usually it swings outward into identification with the body, sensations, feelings, thoughts, and all the complex self-portraits we paint with that palette. But it can also swing inward into nonidentification. When we let it do that, simple, formless, nonidentified awareness spontaneously reveals itself. When the old thoughts of identification arise, just recognize them as nothing but thoughts. Then, in its own time, the true I that has been here all along, hidden in plain sight, comes into focus: empty, luminous, and . . . *ahhhhhhh!* It's just nothing, but there's something very, very, very, *very* good about it.

Think back a moment to your late teens, a time when most of us try on various identities. We might decide to be a party animal, or an aloof intellectual, or a badass biker, or a soulful singer-songwriter, or a disdainful hipster. But, of course, we're none of the identities we try on: we're the one who tries them on. They're roles, often modeled after—ahem!—role models. They're like costumes, patched together out of attitudes and images borrowed from the cool kids and the media: assumed manners, gestures, hairstyles, outfits, even tones of voice. ("Dude!") After *Rebel Without a Cause* came out, with James Dean cool as hell in that red jacket with the turned-up collar, they couldn't keep those jackets in the stores. There's nothing wrong with roles and styles, as long as we don't confuse them with what we are. If we're interested in looking deeper, we follow Maharaj's advice: "Get rid of all ideas about yourself. . . . No self-definition is valid." Then see what remains.

When you first start to meditate in this way, you may have the thought, "But there's nothing to rest *in*. When I used the breath or a sound or the heart center, there was no question about the vehicle. There was a clear object." You're right. Now there's *no* object—only the subject, the witness of all objects. In the old texts, this has been compared to the way a turtle withdraws its limbs into its shell. That's what makes this I-meditation fundamentally different from the others. It's what makes it arguably the most advanced form of meditation as well as the simplest.

Anytime you find yourself wondering, "Wait, where *is* that I?" it's the very awareness that's aware of the question. Look no further. If you try to get rid of it, you'll see that you can't. When you search for it, you're like a fish swimming this way and that, asking, "Where's this ocean I keep hearing about?"

As Mooji has explained,

Only this needs to be recognized: You are looking *for* something, but you are already looking *from* there. Stay with this recognition.

As you do so, you may realize that our simple instruction for this meditation—*Rest in the I-sense*—should be even simpler. Because the I is not something separate from us, we don't have to *sense* it, or rest *in* it, or even *rest*. So instead we can say,

Remain as the I—as you already are.

∾

Once upon a time, a little musk deer was wandering through the forest with his mother. Suddenly he noticed a lovely scent—the sweetest, most alluring scent he had ever smelled. Enchanted, he left his mother's side to follow the scent through the forest, searching for its source. He had to find out where it came from. He sniffed the flowers, the shrubs, the trees, the rocks, the streams, the other animals, but couldn't find its origin. One day, having investigated everything in the forest, he came to its edge, then proceeded into the unknown precincts of the wider world, still on his quest.

Years went by. His search took him to all the continents, all the way around the world. Finally he found himself back in the forest, exhausted and near death from his long journey. He staggered into a familiar-looking clearing. There he found his now aged mother and collapsed at her feet. With his waning breath, he told her of his long, fruitless journey. At last his mother said, "Ah, you poor thing. Don't you understand? You're a *musk* deer. That beautiful scent is your own."

That's the story of our lives, as expounded in an Indian wisdom tale. We've gone from one experience to another, searching for the bliss that was the nature of the experienc*er* all along. Only some temporary confusion, in which a body or a personality was mistaken for I, needs to be seen through. The I that we've always looked *from* turns out to be what we were looking *for*. The scent of the musk deer is the same as the One Taste, the deliciousness of life that we instinctively seek in every moment, till sooner or later we discover that "Tag—you're it!"

It's not that Joe or Jane finally experiences the infinite, but that the infinite—I—drops the pretense that it was ever Joe or Jane. Then we can witness any amount of intensity—orgasm, throat cancer, roller coaster—and none of it disturbs what we are. All manner of fireworks can dance in the surface of the mirror, and the infinitely OK, nothin'-happenin' depths of the mirror remain undisturbed. Whatever's happening may rock or suck, but *I'm* fine. I am I.

Don't believe any of this. Confirm it in your own experience.

~

In the Sanskrit of ancient India, this recognition that the seeker and the sought have never been separate is called *Advaita* (uh-DVAHY-tuh)—"not two," nonduality. The great pioneer of Advaita self-investigation was Adi Shankara, a brilliant sage who traveled throughout the subcontinent, sharing his discovery, in the eighth century (or possibly earlier; accounts differ). Like Jesus, the Buddha, and other great spiritual reformers, he challenged the prevailing custom of merely performing outer rituals and pointed to the simple inner encounter with one's own essence. In later centuries, however, this experiential directness was largely lost, and Advaita was institutionalized into a lifelong program of study and effort. Self-knowledge was declared difficult to attain—a self-fulfilling prophecy.

Then, at the end of the nineteenth century, another reformer came along, this time a sixteen-year-old boy from a village in south India. One day he was suddenly gripped with fear and thought he was dying. But instead of panicking, he lay down on his back in imitation of a corpse, and began the kind of investigation we've been doing here—but stoked by a sense of life-or-death urgency. By observing closely, he saw that he was not the perishable body but the deathless, silent awareness that witnesses the comings and goings of the body and all else that is perishable. And his seeing was so complete and clear that it was not just a fleeting glimpse but full, irreversible self-realization: enlightenment.

Within weeks, the boy left home, made his way to the pilgrimage town of Tiruvanamalai, and climbed Arunachala, the fabled "hill of fire," where holy men had made their home for centuries. There he sat in a cave for seven years, steeping in the bliss of the I-awareness. The local sadhus named him Sri Ramana Maharshi and eventually coaxed him down to the bottom of the hill, where they built an *ashram* for him. He taught there for the rest of his life, drawing seekers from all over the world, cutting through all their confusion with three words:

Who am I?

He advised students to employ that question insistently, unsparingly—not as a topic of intellectual speculation, but as a spur to direct the attention inward to its own source. Asking "Who am I?" is like asking "What color is the sky?" It's not a cue to think, but an invitation to *look*—to lo and behold. And again, it's not a thing we look *at*, but an awakening to the formless awareness we look *from*.

In the next generation, Sri Ramana's teaching of this radical shortcut, which he called *self-inquiry*, was carried on by his disciple H. W. Poonja, known as Papaji. (In India, the suffix *-ji* indicates affection and respect.) Papaji was a brilliant, unpredictable teacher, lanky and bald, with a wide grin and eyes that twinkled with love and mischief. Several of his students continue to teach today. One of them, a Jamaican artist named Tony Moo who quickly gained realization under Papaji's guidance, became known as Mooji, and for the last few decades has been sharing self-inquiry with students all over the world, through his travels and on YouTube.

Yaffa and I first met Mooji in 2008 at a retreat in southern Italy, way down in the heel of the boot, in an old, weathered villa, nestled among the olive groves outside the historic city of Lecce. The retreat was to start that evening. It was a hot day in late June, and we had traveled by plane, train, bus, and car to arrive at this remote spot. We dropped our bags inside and were led out to a verandah where Mooji was relaxing on an old couch with a blue cover, chatting with two or three students in his deep bass-baritone voice with its soft island lilt. Brown skin. Long dreads. Black beard starting to go gray at the chin. A plain cotton Indian shirt. A stocky frame with forearms like tree trunks and thick fingers on powerful hands. A massive skull like an elephant's, or Ganesha's, and faintly Asian-looking eyes (from his Chinese father), which shone with clear, deep, luminous compassion. He welcomed us, we sat down with him on the couch, he took both of our hands. . . .

And then something happened. The sun beat down, and the hot, dry breeze stirred the olive trees. Some chatting continued, but I don't know what was said or who said it. My eyes might have been open or closed. From somewhere in the distance came the sound of music, or voices, I can't say. What I can say is that time fell away, space fell away, all sense of *you* and *I* fell away, as if a rug had been pulled out from under us . . . and then the floor . . . and then the earth. Everything fell away. What was left in its place was boundlessness, and it was the most natural thing in the world.

After a lifetime of encountering some truly wonderful, enlightened teachers, I knew I had found one who—at least for me—is more than a teacher, someone who embodies the infinite, breathes it, radiates it, *is* it, while speaking and acting and laughing in the most down-to-earth, matter-of-fact way imaginable. Later, Yaffa and I compared notes and found that we had both experienced the same thing: this is what it must have been like to sit with the Buddha, Shankara, Ramana, Jesus, any of the great sages of old. Now we understood the power they had, just by the clarity of their silent presence, to ignite the spark of enlightenment in others . . . at least in those who were open to receive that ignition, from that teacher, at that time. (Your mileage may vary.)

It was a great retreat, by the way. There were some fifty of us, all crammed into the little villa or sleeping in tents on the surrounding grounds, sharing three bathrooms. Most of the retreatants were Italians, who smoked everywhere and couldn't maintain silence between sessions to save their lives. The cook was Italian too, and the food was delicious.

We had two long sessions with Mooji each day, mostly devoted to *satsang* (SUT-sung), "association with the truth." This is a kind of enlightened Socratic dialogue, in which students present their questions and doubts and the teacher leads them out of their perplexity. Satsang is often full of surprises. In frustration, a student might say something like, "You insist that I'm already infinite beingness. But I'm not *experiencing* it." The teacher, refusing to get entangled in the "it" at the end of the sentence (some phenomenon the student is looking *for*) might direct the student's attention to the "I" at the beginning of the sentence (where he's looking *from*): "And who is this I that doesn't experience it?" Each time the student tries to turn the I into an object or a concept, the teacher deftly undermines that attempt—or suddenly blows it up, as the occasion demands. Watching Mooji conduct satsang is like watching a chess master press his opponent till he runs out of moves, or like watching a skilled surgeon at work, peeling back the layers of tissue, finally revealing the heart. This heart, the heart of the matter, is boundless awareness. The scalpel is Ramana's unsparing question: *Who am I?*

Sitting meditation is still part of the program. But we've already seen how thin and porous the membrane between "meditation" and "life" can become. With this inquiry into the formless Self, the membrane dissolves completely. Instructions can become minimal. Sri Ramana gave concise meditation instructions like, *Remain as you are* or *Let what comes come, let what goes go, see what remains.*

Papaji's famous, oft-repeated instruction was *Just keep quiet.* ("But Papaji, what about—" "Just keep quiet.") Mooji has said it many different ways, including, *Don't use your mind to try and figure things out. What is it that watches your mind? Be there—now.* Or simply *Stay as the Self.*

~

Finally, it's all very simple. Meditation? Remain as the I, presence, consciousness, not caught up in identifying with anything else. Self-inquiry? Remain as the I, presence, consciousness, not caught up in identifying with anything else. Living your life? Same same. Mooji has put it succinctly:

There is only awareness, no "one" being aware.

Just put this to the test. If you find out it's true, you're done.

If this kind of nonpractice practice seems too steep, too simple, you can always go back to the breath or the heart center or something else with a well-defined handle you can grab hold of. But at some point come back here. Your Self is calling you.

When you find yourself caught up or overwhelmed by something—work stress, an emotionally charged situation, a bedeviling thought, whatever—you can "follow the bad smell back," as Mooji puts it. That is, rather than suppressing it or wallowing in it, use the situation of experienc*ing* to trace your way back to the experienc*er*. Who is it that's stressed? Who am I? Follow the stress (or the confusion, or grief—or happiness) back to the I that witnesses it. At last you can retire from the endless task of trying to chase all the sadness from your life or hang on to all the happiness. You still experience human emotions—in fact, for the first time you experience them without inhibition—but they're dwarfed by the vastness of what you are.

Just leaning in this direction, Vespa-like, can lift a tremendous weight off our lives. But many people never seriously consider these fundamental questions till they're hit with something dire: an illness, a ruptured marriage, a kid on drugs. For such situations, Mooji once presented a little A/B test:

> Experiment a little. Take this attitude: In any given situation, look from the position or standpoint of the personal "I" and observe the inner response. Now switch. Identify "I" only as consciousness and feel the difference. Choose the position you wish to be in.

~

It may have occurred to you that, if we're all really boundless, skylike being-awareness rather than individual persons, then we must all be the *same* skylike being-awareness. (Then the Beatles were right when they sang, "I am he as you are he as you are me / And we are all together.") How can there be two skies? Everything that made us seem separate belongs to the realm of bodies, thoughts, boundaries. On the level of Advaita, nondual truth, there can be no separation because there are no two to be separated. "We're all one" turns out to be not just a hippie cliché but a straightforward description of our actual situation.

Yaffa and I met each other shortly before we met Mooji. For three years, we carried on a long-distance romance, three thousand miles apart. It was a perfect opportunity to put this teaching to the test. We were highly motivated to find the space in which we were not two and therefore not separate, no matter where our bodies happened to be. We might be on our opposite coasts for three weeks, then together for a weekend, then apart again. Together, apart, together, apart. Like turning your head to the left and then to the right: two different situations, but what remains the same? After a while, that became pretty clear. When one of us did fly out to visit the other, it was wonderful and blissful and easeful and romantic and exciting, and also kind of . . . superfluous.

I eventually threw in the towel and moved to California. (She was sure as hell not gonna move to New Jersey.) We got married, and our life together was—is—based in that which remains always the same, that invisible essence. We know that someday our nonseparateness will be put to a harder test, the final exam, when our bodies are separated by death.

Of course, every couple in love knows that this challenge awaits them. For some, that knowledge may be the spur to find out *Who am I?* OK. Whatever it takes.

22. The Door Is Everywhere

Yaffa and I had read that floating in a houseboat down the backwaters of Kerala, in southwestern India, is one of the fifty things to do before you die. Now we were doing it, and it was true. We had hired one of the many beautiful boats lined up at the Alleppey docks, with an above-decks structure of bamboo poles and woven palm leaves, and a three-man crew that was expert in making themselves scarce, almost invisible, as they sailed. Slowly, soundlessly, the boat glided along the inland waterway, past thick jungles, rice paddies, and occasional villages where the people still live much as they have for centuries. Now and then we'd see a man up to his neck in the water, holding on to a long pole, hunting shellfish by the traditional method; or we'd pass through an impossibly huge flock of ducks, thousands of ducks, what seemed like every duck in the world. Women washing their clothes ignored us or flashed broad smiles. Children waved or danced.

As the sun set and the sky behind the black-silhouetted palm trees flooded with red, the cook materialized, carrying a tray with a pot of chai, cups, and saucers, then discreetly vanished once again. In the distance, jungle birds called to one another. We sipped our chai in silence.

Finally, Yaffa set down her cup and said, "Well? Should we do our evening meditation?"

It took a moment for her words to register. Then we both burst out laughing. Everything was so ridiculously tranquil that the idea of changing anything to "meditate," whatever that might mean—moving a muscle, shifting a limb, closing or opening an eye—seemed completely, hilariously redundant.

The next day we got off the boat at Thottappally, but now, seven years later, we both have a sense that we never completely disembarked. In time, our whole life is becoming that houseboat ride.

This is what eventually happens to anyone who does natural meditative practice with some persistence. When meditation really works, it makes meditation obsolete.

~

The Buddha used his own nautical metaphor to express the same thing:

> My teaching is a means of practice, not something to hold on to or worship. My teaching is like a raft used to cross the river. Only a fool would carry the raft around after he had already reached the far shore of liberation.

All the meditation, all the methods, the mantras, books, insights, experiences, all have just one purpose: to make it easier to see what was there all along, the delicious, liberative nature of existence itself. Once they've served that purpose, you can let them go.

But don't burn your raft too soon.

We started this book by seeing why people don't stick to meditation—usually because they're forcing it, trying to control the mind. When you've been grinding away like that, stopping is thoroughly sensible: forcing hurts, and it doesn't work.

But some people drift away from the practice precisely because it does work. They start seeing through the old belief that they're an isolated object, a person, an ego zipped inside a bag of skin. Of course such disillusionment is the luckiest fate that can ever befall us, but after so many years of perfecting our role, we may have some resistance to finding out at the end of our movie that—spoiler alert!—it's just a movie.

Ego—the sense of a separate, constricted self—doesn't want to be knocked off the throne it usurped so long ago; and mind, the bogus king's prime minister, will invent all sorts of creative ways to block awareness, the rightful ruler, from being restored to the throne. Mind can provide an endless supply of reasons not to practice, from the trivial ("Wait, just one more email!") to the epic (elaborate philosophical arguments). Most excuses fall somewhere in between: "It's not in tune with my personal journey this month" or "Big project this week . . . so much buzzing around in my head . . . I'll meditate when things lighten up." Nope. Things will lighten up when you meditate.

This is worth repeating: it's really, really good to have a habit of regular, daily sitting practice—even if it's for just one minute. Once you're in that yummy soup, and are reminded yet again why you started this stuff in the first place, you'll probably stay longer, but even if you don't, you've already made the difference. You've given yourself one more booster shot, the live virus of spaciousness that reinoculates you against the claustrophobia of being an ego.

There are lovely, poetic models for this kind of commitment. Jesus had his forty days and forty nights of fasting in the wilderness. Siddhartha Gautama, after six years of meditative practice, was on the verge of becoming the Awakener—the Buddha. Sitting at the foot of a great fig tree, he vowed,

> Though my skin, my nerves, and my bones shall waste away and my life blood go dry, I will not leave this seat until I have attained the highest wisdom, called supreme enlightenment, that leads to everlasting happiness.

As he meditated, it is said, he was assailed by every hallucinatory delusion the mind and ego could devise, from fearsome, elephant-mounted warriors to naked dancing girls. But he refused to budge, and in the hour before dawn—as Venus, the beautiful morning star, rose in the east—he attained final liberation.

Inspired by such examples, it does seem reasonable that we should be able to manage a few minutes a day on the commuter train . . . or after we put the kids to bed . . . or before reaching once again for the remote. . . .

~

Still, meditation is not an end in itself. It's not a destination. It's a door into boundless being. If we use it skillfully, we see that sitting back and enjoying a cup of coffee is also the door. Making love or being stuck in rush-hour traffic is also the door. Health and illness are the door. India is the door and Nebraska is the door. All acts of religious ritual are the door, as are all other acts. Laughing at any time is the door. ("It is good that we can laugh like this," Mooji once said, "because when you laugh you cannot think.") As I wrap up this book, I'm still sitting in the garden, but the mockingbirds and hummingbirds are gone. There's a busted sewer line under the street in front of the house next door, and there's been equipment and guys in hardhats there for two weeks now. The roar of the backhoe and the beeping backup signals of the trucks are also the door. The door is everywhere.

In the tea ceremony of Japan and other East Asian cultures, the mundane acts of brewing, serving, pouring, and drinking are elevated to sacred ritual: the infinite shows through each ordinary finite action. Eventually, everything—washing the dishes, tying your shoes—is tea ceremony. Earlier we quoted Arturo Sandoval, advising us to thank God that we're practicing instead of breaking stones or driving a truck. But once your practice fulfills its purpose, you can thank God that you *are* driving a truck. What could be better?

This tea ceremony principle is beautifully depicted in what is probably my favorite painting in the world, Vermeer's *Milkmaid*. Actually depicting a kitchen maid pouring a thin trickle of milk from a large jug, it shows what it's like to act in this same-old same-old world with your brand-new, boundary-melting awareness. Our crisp, sharp-focused, high-def experience of the finite is suggested by the minutely, almost photorealistically rendered textures of the objects surrounding the maid: the coarse surfaces of the bread (some of which is visibly turning stale), the market basket and copper pail hanging by the window, the nail holes in the wall behind her.

But the maid herself—that is, the flesh of her bare forearms and face—is painted in a smoothed-over, washed-out, almost abstract style,

Vermeer's *Milkmaid*

suggesting that, at the hub of all perceived objects, with all their qualities and colors, is the colorless, qualityless, objectless perceiver. Behind her (as X-ray analysis has shown), Vermeer originally hung a large wall map, but he wisely painted it out later, leaving her backed instead by a bare, sun-washed wall—a vacancy in place of the world, a naturalistic halo of just-nothing-but-something-very-good-about-it. The maid's facial expression has been compared to that of the enigmatic Mona Lisa. But as her head bows to her task in silent, natural, utterly relaxed concentration, with her eyes downcast and her wide forehead lit by the same pale golden light that illuminates the wall—the same light within you and without you—she's really a Buddha.

Apparently, the maid is making bread pudding, pouring fresh milk (the only bit of pure white on the canvas) from the dark recesses of the jug onto the stale bread. In the same way, pure, ever-fresh, all-nurturing awareness constantly pours forth from the invisible recesses of our deepest interior and onto the once-stale daily bread of mundane experience. The result of this kitchen alchemy is a perpetual transformation. Every moment, no matter how routine and ordinary, becomes, like pudding, rich and delicious.

At the beginning of this book, we talked about the rare, perfect ahhhhhhh moments of life. Because they're so precious and so fleeting, most people try to hold on to them, dwelling in their scrapbooks and stories, even as the fresh, new moment—this one! now this one!—fleets by unnoticed. But now, as we discover that *every* moment is a perfect ahhhhhhh, we can let each one go as we welcome the next, loving the one we're with, finally fulfilling William Blake's great prophecy:

> *He who kisses the joy as it flies*
> *Lives in eternity's sunrise.*

Then formal, "official" sitting meditation becomes less crucial, as everything you do becomes informal, unofficial, spontaneous sitting-standing-walking-dreaming-working-playing meditation. Since natural meditation was always a matter of just being rather than doing, this makes perfect sense. Making a salad is meditation: You're just being, tearing the lettuce. Then you're just being, slicing the tomatoes, or rather, you're just being slicing *this* tomato, *this* slice. Adding the olives is eternity's sunrise. Then pouring the oil is eternity's sunrise. All the moments of making the salad are just as good as all the moments of eating the salad. Maybe the hurricane or the heart attack will strike first, and you'll never get to eat it. That will be eternity's sunrise as well.

Most people have probably had the dream of suddenly finding a door in their house to a room they somehow didn't know they'd had all along. I suspect that this is what that dream is about. Brushing your teeth is the door to infinity. Walking your dog is the door to infinity. Waking and sleeping, living and dying: everything is the door. It's all meditation, and there's no such thing as meditation. Meditation isn't, acclimation is. Now we're acclimating to the discovery that every inch of our finite existence is the infinite; every note of our song is the shimmering, heart-opening, sky-filling technicolor silence.

And it's all perfectly natural and ordinary. From the outside, you might look about the same as other people, except that you don't complain a lot, and the others feel mysteriously relaxed just being around you. You see their perfect beauty, but you know better than to try to tell them about it before they have ears to hear. It's not as if something has finally been set right, but simply that the bad dream that something was wrong has dropped away.

Before, we searched for the Promised Land. Now we see that we *are* the Promised Land.

Before, hearing the tantalizing descriptions of nirvana or the kingdom of heaven, we were like a carful of children on our way to the sea for the first time, imploring Dad every five minutes, "Are we there yet?" But now that we're here, looking out over all that vastness, it's as if the journey never happened.

Acknowledgments

Thank you to Alison Ellwood, Howard Geer, Howard Leder, Sean Nolan, and Carl Norman, who all read sections of early drafts and made helpful suggestions. Yaffa Lerea brought her exceptional sense of rhythm and clarity, and her deep understanding of What's What, to bear on the whole book at several stages.

Shayna Hiller, a wonderful teacher of yoga and more, kindly posed for photos.

My publisher, Joel Fotinos, set me on course to write this book and provided wisdom and vision in guiding it into its present form; without him it would not exist. Gaby Moss served as both sharp, sensitive editor and brave test-driver, my ideal newbie meditator. When she graduated from her day job, Andrew Yackira heroically batted cleanup. Thanks also to all the behind-the-scenes folks at Tarcher in departments like design, copyediting, and marketing, who turn bunches of words into beautiful books and get them into your hands.

I am deeply grateful to my students, my friends, my sangha brothers and sisters, and my family, near and far, for their encouragement and support in its many forms.

My mother-in-law, Joan Lerea, graciously listened as I read the almost-final manuscript aloud. I received precious silent editorial guidance whenever she laughed, she furrowed her brow, or her eyes sparkled with an *Aha!* of understanding. This book is much better thanks to her. On the day that I was to read her the final installment—after she had already heard a lot about letting go into something bigger—she unexpectedly passed away. The sunset that evening was spectacular.

Finally and always, I bow to my Teacher, and to all the kind teachers through whom my Teacher shines.

Photo Credits

Index